Predecessors, Et Cetera

Poets on Poetry   Donald Hall, General Editor

Amy Clampitt

Predecessors, Et Cetera

ESSAYS

Ann Arbor
The University of Michigan Press

Library of Congress Cataloging-in-Publication Data

Clampitt, Amy.
    Predecessors, et cetera : essays / Amy Clampitt.
        p.   cm.—(Poets on poetry)
    Includes bibliographical references.
    ISBN 0-472-09457-2 (cloth : alk.).—ISBN 0-472-06457-6 (paper :
alk.)
    1. American literature—History and criticism.   2. English poetry—
History and criticism.   3. Poetry.   I. Title.   II. Series.
PS121.C5   1991
810.9—dc20   90-28569
                                                                    CIP

British Library Cataloguing in Publication Data

Clampitt, Amy
    Predecessors, et cetera : essays.—(Poets on poetry).
    I. Title   II. Series
    821.009

    ISBN 0-472-09457-2
    ISBN 0-472-06457-6 pbk

Distributed in the United Kingdom and Europe by
Manchester University Press, Oxford Road,
Manchester M13 9PL, UK

for Carl Niemeyer

Author's Note

Writing good prose is never easy. In an interview that appears toward the end of this collection, I am quoted as saying that having gotten to think of myself as a poet, I don't write prose any more. Evidently that is a bit less true than when I said it. The fact remains that writing prose is still, for me, more difficult than writing what I can only hope (but never be sure) is good poetry. There are the underpinnings of syntax, which the levitations and prestidigitations of verse have not only now and then, but famously, dispensed with—the connectives left out, the predications eluded, the conclusions that leave nothing settled. These are strategies not available to the writer of a prose essay. Whereas a poet may get away with being still a child, on the page as elsewhere, one has to at least behave as though one were a grown-up in order to write acceptable prose; and I have had my doubts about being grown up enough to qualify.

Nevertheless, occasions have arisen when the challenge of making the effort proved irresistible: being asked to review a book I might or might not otherwise have read, or to take part in a symposium, or to offer some observations in public. What those occasions have had in common is the opportunity of learning something new by way of reading, ruminating, and putting my particular responses in order. The pieces that follow are offered, diffidently, as no more than that—an experience and a process shared.

Contents

Predecessors, Et Cetera

What do you need to know to be a writer?

My first reaction to the question was, Do I know enough about anything to even be taking part in this conversation?

One of my favorite stories has to do with David Starr Jordan, the first president of Stanford University. Before he became a university president, he was an ichthyologist—he studied fishes. At first, as president of a new college, he made a point of knowing the names of all the students. But he soon gave it up because, he said, every time he learned the name of a student he forgot a fish. Because I've forgotten a lot of fishes, among many other things, that story somehow consoles me.

I'll tell you another story that may shed some light on what a writer needs to know. Lately it was my good fortune to spend some time at Yaddo, a country hideaway with lots of evergreens and a chance to do some bird-watching. I'm not a genuine, certified bird-watcher—I don't keep a life list—but ever since my Aunt Edith pointed out something lovely in a maple tree, when I was maybe four or five years old, and told me it was a rose-breasted grosbeak, knowing the names of birds has seemed a normal thing to do. At Yaddo there was said to be a pileated woodpecker, which alas I never saw. But I did see a fair number of nuthatches and tufted titmice, and lots of chickadees. Does anybody here not know chickadees? I'm not so sure about that as I might have been, because one day I was walking with one of the residents up there, a writer,

---

Originally read at Grinnell College in February, 1986.

and I said something about the chickadees, and he said, "Which are those?"

Well, that did give me pause. If the writer had been a poet, I think I might have said, "Man, you call yourself a poet and you don't know chickadees?" But he wasn't, and I didn't. The truth no doubt was that for the kind of writing he did, he had no need to think about them. And I have to say further that living in New York City, I know people who are bemused by the notion that *anybody* should notice, to the extent of assigning it a name, a very small bird that says "Dee, dee, dee" and hangs around in winter. My best friend happens to be a native New Yorker, and he is vastly entertained by the existence of a thing called a tufted titmouse. But I don't know that he is any more amused than I am by the language people in his profession—he's a lawyer—use without any notion of how funny it sounds to somebody who isn't. Take *tortfeasor*. I don't know how lawyers can say it with a straight face. I once wrote a poem that ended with the word *tortfeasor*—it was about wild mushrooms, some of which can do harm, presumably without really meaning to, which is the case with most tortfeasors— and no editor would take it. Which I suppose must mean that knowledge of such a thing is not anything you need in order to be a writer—or to be a poet anyhow.

If you're going to be a novelist, it appears to me that you need to know an awful lot. By the time I graduated from college, that's what I thought I was going to be. I'd written poetry off and on, but I had no plans to write any more. And I did in fact write novels—three of them all told, none of which, luckily, ever got into print. I'm not sure now precisely when it was settled in my mind that a poet was what, after all, I was going to have to be. I do remember, though, when I realized I was never going to make it as a novelist. It was as I was reading Thomas Pynchon's *The Crying of Lot 49*. It's set in California, where the first tremors of what's in store for the rest of the country seem generally to occur. Pynchon seemed to have picked up those tremors, along with an awesome quantity of detail, some of it trivial, but none of it insignificant, about the way people were living out there. And I realized how hopelessly behind the times I was, and there didn't seem to be much likelihood that I could ever catch up. You know what the Red Queen said to Alice about how in Looking-glass country you had to keep running just to stay in the same place? Well, that's the way I felt. And it occurs to me that that may explain why so many writers of fiction nowadays have taken to setting their stories ahead—so as to have a certain amount of leeway before events catch up with them. Without that leeway, what is a writer to do—especially one who has a constitutional resistance to going so fast all the time? (That's why I stay out of airplanes whenever possible.) The answer is pretty clear: you start looking back. Some novelists do that. Poets all do it— I *think*—at least some of the time.

And here, in case anybody thought I'd never get to it, is where a college education comes in. Or at least that part of a college education generally referred to as the humanities. I think the most precious thing I brought away with me from four years at Grinnell was the beginning of a sense of—how shall I put it?—the livingness of the past. Only the beginning of that sense—but you have to begin somewhere, otherwise it's hard to see how the world we live in can have any meaning, and if one cannot find meaning in the world, it seems to me that living in it at all is no more than just bearable. The chief eye-opener among the courses I took at Grinnell was one on the history of art, taught by a wonderful woman named Edith Sternfeld. One thing it meant to me was that when I got to Europe for the first time, I knew something of what to pay attention to, and occasionally even what to be startled by. I remember riding on a train through the south of France and suddenly realizing that a wild plant I'd seen through the window was an acanthus—a spiny, shiny plant with intricately cutout leaves, very beautiful in its spiny, shiny, intricate way; but what made me keep looking was realizing that from the time of the Greeks some version of that cut out leaf had gotten into the design of the capitals on Corinthian columns, and into painting as well. Once you've had it pointed out to you, that motif turns out to be everywhere. But it came from a wild plant. Is any of this important enough to have gotten so excited about? Who can say? For me, it's the essence of what makes the world an interesting place—and I stress it because what I see from my own peculiar perspective, as a writer of poetry, is a conspiracy all around to stamp out the sense of living continuity, to stamp out singularity, to do away with everything that's not a recognizable commodity, and in the process to make ordinary day-to-day living as *boring* as possible. That's only my opinion, but if I didn't hold it, I wouldn't be a writer. Even if I weren't a writer, unless I'd been totally anesthetized by the boringness of living in a world made up entirely of commodities, I hope I'd still be tuning in on the kind of experience I had a couple of days ago. On my way out here, I made a stopover in Lancaster, Pennsylvania, where I'd been invited by a friend who knows the kind of thing I like taking notice of: he'd told me that though it was a little early in the season, just maybe—since that part of Pennsylvania happens to be on a migratory flyway—I'd hear the geese passing over on their way north. So there was a certain amount of banter about what my friend had halfway promised. But do you know what? I'd made my appearance, and we were just coming out into the snow—into the *snow,* mind you—and my friend said, "Listen!"—and there they were, the geese honking as they passed overhead! It was the first time I'd heard that sound, I think, since I was a child on the farm—but I've thought of it often, and I've watched geese in flight and tried to write about how they looked. And I suppose always in the back of my mind were the geese who were the chief mentors of the young Arthur in *The Once and Future King.* There is, by the way, another book of T. H. White's, less well known, that I think I love even more: *The Goshawk,* about his experience as a would-be falconer. Is any of this important? It is if you agree with Wallace Stevens that the worst poverty is not to live in a physical world. I might paraphrase that and say that for me it would be a terrible deprivation to live in a world that took no notice of the migration of geese or of the ways of goshawks, falcons, kestrels . . .

Last summer I was in England, doing some of the little jobs a writer now and then gets to do, and the really high point, the greatest moment of that entire summer came during a weekend I spent on a farm in Dorset. One morning I came down to breakfast and found one of the teenage boys in the family with two kestrels (they'd been injured, and he was training them to hunt for themselves) perched on the back of a kitchen chair. To be that close to a wild bird of any kind is rare enough, but what made the occasion electric was that another name for kestrel is—the *windhover.*

> I caught this morning morning's minion, king-
> dom of daylight's dauphin, dapple-dawn-drawn Falcon . . .

Like the sight of the acanthus growing wild, the sight of those kestrels, those windhovers, was all the more precious because, years before, I'd discovered the poetry of Gerard Manley Hopkins. I can't be sure I'd ever have become a poet if I had never been introduced to his poems—but in any event I find it impossible to imagine the kind of poet I would have been if I hadn't. It's like imagining a world in which one's own parents had never met.

What does a writer need to know? In one word, I'd say, predecessors. I don't know why it is that things become more precious with the awareness that someone else has looked at them, thought about them, written about them. But so I find it to be. There is less originality than we think. There is also a vast amount of solitude. Writers need company. We all need it. It's not the command of knowledge that matters finally, but the company. It's the predecessors. As a writer, I don't know where I'd be without them.

Wordsworth in 1990

It takes an effort, even now, not to think of William Words-worth as an eminence and a dodderer, the consummate Poet Laureate. But he didn't become Poet Laureate until he was in his seventies, long after his real work as a poet was done. Reading Stephen Gill's new biography, *William Wordsworth: A Life* (Oxford, 1989), I have been struck by the degree to which he was, and indeed remains, controversial. For three decades, from around 1790 to 1820, he had been anything but a member of the literary establishment—unless it was as an established laughingstock. In the year 1820, when he published *The River Duddon,* the tide turned, and reviewers began applying all the lavish terms they had so long withheld. Back in 1807, Lord Byron had found Wordsworth's *Poems, in Two Volumes* "commonplace," "namby-pamby," and "puerile." Francis Jeffrey, who could be thought of as the Hilton Kramer of his day, described the same collection as "silly," "tedious," and "affected." According to Jared Curtis in his introduction to the Cornell edition,

> Jeffrey in a letter to Henry Hallam (October 1807) pretended that it went against his "conscience" to attack Wordsworth's poetry a second time in his *Edinburgh Review;* in fact, he carried out what he jokingly called his "plan" to "lay a few strokes on Wordsworth," setting the tone and point of view for much of the criticism of *Poems, in Two Volumes,* for many years afterward.

Adapted from an informal address at The New York Public Library on March 8, 1990.

Whatever the state of his conscience when Wordsworth brought out *The Excursion* seven years later, Jeffrey responded with the opening sentence, the death sentence, for which he is now mainly remembered. "This will never do," he wrote, and proceeded to round out a page-long indictment with: "The case of Mr. Wordsworth is now manifestly hopeless; and we give him up as altogether incurable, and beyond the power of criticism." But still he couldn't leave the subject alone. And what he went on to say was the more awful, for the victim anyhow, in that some of it (such as the charge of abstruseness and prolixity) was undeniable; and then there was the praise ("occasional gleams of tenderness and beauty") which leaves the victim of a hostile review writhing under a show of impeccable fairness and restraint. There is no doubt that unlike some others, who merely enjoyed poking fun, Francis Jeffrey *was* hostile. He was so because he sincerely believed Wordsworth's ideas were dangerous. Take these lines from "The Old Cumberland Beggar":

> . . . the poorest poor
> Long for some moments in a weary life
> When they can know and feel that they have been
> Themselves the fathers and the dealers out
> Of some small blessings, have been kind to such
> As needed kindness, for this single cause,
> That we have all of us one human heart.

That last line might sound unobjectionable.* But wait a minute. Begging was a subject on which Wordsworth had strong views. Earlier in this same poem he addressed the "Statesmen! Ye / Who have a broom still ready in your hands / To rid the world of nuisances"—and a year or so later, writing to one of those same statesmen, he declared that he had aimed in more than one poem "to shew that men who do not wear fine cloaths can feel deeply."

---

*Objection has been made to this passage on the ground implicit in Auden's withering gloss on the maxim that we are "here to help others": "I don't know what the others are for."

Again, that might pass for a truism. But let no one suppose it unarguable. Much debate led up to, and much discussion followed, a ruling by Judge Leonard Sand, early this year, giving beggars leave to make their pitch on a New York subway platform. The opinion was predicated on the constitutional right of free speech. The ground of Wordsworth's concern for the old Cumberland beggar and his like was other, and far less novel: it was the perennially troublesome belief in the value of every human soul.

"That we have all of us one human heart": I thought of this when Nelson Mandela came out of a South African jail, and the *New York Times* reprinted parts of a speech he had made from the prisoner's dock in 1964, before he was sentenced to life imprisonment. On that day Mandela had spoken of how "when anything has to be carried or cleaned the white man will look around for an African to do it for him, whether the African is employed by him or not," so that whites tended to regard Africans as a separate breed, "and not to recognize them as having the same emotions" as themselves. What was being denied in South Africa was, in other words, "that we have all one human heart."

And not only in South Africa. According to Francis Jeffrey's view, "The love, or grief, or indignation of an enlightened and refined character is . . . in itself a different emotion from the love, or grief, or anger, of a clown [that is, a country-dweller], a tradesman, or a market-wench." This is from his review of *Lyrical Ballads,* which he chose to regard as the manifesto of a "*sect*" of poets, "*dissenters* from the established systems of poetry and criticism," who were guilty of "a splenetic and idle discontent with the existing institutions of society."

As a "sect," the so-called Lake Poets didn't amount to much. There was Coleridge, who whatever his earlier views was already on the side of the establishment. There was Southey, who had been even quicker to shed the subversive follies of his youth. There was De Quincey, who wrote in prose, and had been a Tory from the start. No, it was Wordsworth whom Jeffrey meant to attack, because he saw him as a threat to the maintenance of public order. Never mind that Wordsworth had expressed, in his preface to the very book that worried

Jeffrey so, his own alarm that "a multitude of causes, unknown to former times, are now acting with a combined force to blunt the discriminating powers of the mind, and unfitting it for all voluntary exertion to reduce it to a state of almost savage torpor." And he might have been writing in 1990, not in 1800, when he deplored "the encreasing accumulation of men in cities, where the uniformity of their occupation produces a craving for extraordinary incident, which the rapid communication of intelligence hourly gratifies."

Sixteen years later, things in England looked even worse. A prime minister had been assassinated; there were food riots; the Luddites were smashing up machinery in the provinces. Wordsworth by then had begun to sound scared in more nearly the way Jeffrey was scared. He wrote to a friend that

> the lower orders have been for upwards of thirty years accumulating in pestilential masses of ignorant population; the effects now begin to show themselves, and unthinking people cry out that the national character has been changed all at once, in fact the change has been silently going on ever since the time they were born; the disease has been growing, and breaks out in all its danger and deformity.

There can be no doubt that as Wordsworth got older, reaction set in. His later political views are clearly those of a Tory. George Ticknor, the Boston publisher, reported after a visit to Rydal Mount:

> He holds . . . to the old and established in the institutions, usages, and peculiarities of his country, and he sees them all shaken by the progress of change. His moral sensibilities are offended. . . . But he talks without bitterness. . . . He was very curious, too, about our institutions in America . . . ; but is certainly not inclined to augur well of our destinies, for he goes upon the broad principle that the mass of people cannot be trusted with the powers of government.

But even as he opposed giving the "lower orders" the vote, Wordsworth continued to insist on the common passions of humankind. "If my writings are to last," he wrote to his friend

Henry Crabb Robinson, "it will I myself believe be mainly owing to this. They will please for a single cause, 'That we have all one human heart!' "

That was Wordsworth in 1835. His greatest poems, with one notable exception, had all been written. The exception is his "Extempore Effusion upon the Death of James Hogg." Its ostensible subject had been no more than an acquaintance; but hearing late that year that the "Ettrick Shepherd" was dead seems to have opened the way for feelings until then repressed. The poem moves from a roll of the departed into a lament for the greatest of them, who had long ago been his greatest friend:

> Nor has the rolling year twice measured,
> From sign to sign, its steadfast course,
> Since every mortal power of Coleridge
> Was frozen at its marvellous source;
>
> The rapt One, of the godlike forehead,
> The heaven-eyed creature sleeps in earth . . . .

It was as though, after so many years, what had sprung from no more than a blank misgiving—

> No motion has she now, no force,
> She neither hears nor sees,
> Rolled round in earth's diurnal course,
> With rocks, and stones, and trees—

had revealed its entire significance, and in the long-ago-apprehended burden of the mystery there now lay the accumulated weight of a lifetime. It could be said that here, like Masha in *The Seagull*, Wordsworth was in mourning for his life.

Think of him in 1790, writing his sister of a nation "mad with joy," of

> France standing on the top of golden hours,
> And human nature seeming born again.

It is as though, two centuries later, we were seeing that joy come home, week after week, as we watched the evening news: first in Leipzig, then at the Brandenburg Gate, then in Wenceslas Square—and also in Tiananmen Square, before we knew how the rejoicing there would end. Of that kind of rejoicing, in all its feverish evanescence, no one has given a more moving account than Wordsworth, who with his friend Robert Jones had landed at Calais on the first anniversary of the fall of the Bastille, and seen

> In a mean City, and among a few,
> How bright a face is worn when joy of one
> Is joy of tens of millions. Southward thence
> We took our way direct through Hamlets, Towns,
> Gaudy with reliques of that Festival,
> Flowers left to wither on triumphal Arcs,
> And window-Garlands. On the public roads,
> And once three days successively through paths
> By which our toilsome journey was abridged,
> Among sequestered villages we walked,
> And found benevolence and blessedness
> Spread like a fragrance everywhere, like Spring
> That leaves no corner of the Land untouched.

Of course the spring does not last. This is Wordsworth's own haunted and recurring theme:

> Spring returns,
> I saw the Spring return, when I was dead
> To deeper hope, yet had I joy for her,
> And welcomed her benevolence, rejoiced
> In common with the Children of her Love. . . .

Having ourselves seen something like that spring return, we in 1990 are bound to read and reread Wordsworth a little differently. Having ourselves witnessed what happened in Tiananmen Square is to shudder with him as he wrote, re-membering, of how "the scenes that I witnessed during the earlier years of the French Revolution, when I was resident in France, come back to me with appalling violence." The inner turmoil those scenes aroused is set down in the tenth book of what we know as *The Prelude*, but which Wordsworth always referred to as the Poem to Coleridge:

Most melancholy at that time, O Friend!
Were my day-thoughts, my dreams were miserable;
Through months, through years, long after the last beat
Of those atrocities (I speak here truth,
As if to thee alone in private talk)
I scarcely had one night of quiet sleep,
Such ghastly visions had I of despair
And tyranny, and implements of death,
And long orations which in dreams I pleaded
Before unjust tribunals, with a voice
Labouring, a brain confounded, and a sense,
Of treachery and desertion in the place,
The holiest that I knew of, my own soul.

It is the kind of passage Keats might have been thinking of when he wrote to John Hamilton Reynolds: "We feel the 'burden of the Mystery.' To this point was Wordsworth come, as far as I can conceive when he wrote 'Tintern Abbey' and it seems to me that his Genius is exploration of those dark Passages."

But of course Keats never saw *The Prelude*, or knew of its existence; and the resolve in that same letter—"Now if we live, and go on thinking we too shall explore them"—becomes the more poignant, and his depth and acuity as a critic the more remarkable, when it is remembered that he wrote all this before he was twenty-three. He would by then have read *The Excursion*, and pronounced it one of the "three things to rejoice at in this Age" (the others being Hazlitt's lectures and the paintings of B. R. Haydon, whose reputation has fared less well). In an early sonnet, Keats had already paid conscious tribute:

Great Spirits now on Earth are sojourning
He of the Cloud the Cataract the Lake
Who on Helvellyn's summit wide awake
Catches his freshness from Archangel's wing. . . .

And he had offered the further tribute of perhaps unconscious allusion to *The Excursion*. Wordsworth's lines,

> Society became my glittering bride,
> And airy hopes my children
> (Book III, 734–35)

seem to glimmer upside down, like a reflection, in this cadenza from a letter Keats wrote to his brother and sister-in-law in America:

> Though . . . the Wine [were] beyond Claret, the Window opening on Winander mere, I should not feel—or rather my Happiness would not be so fine, as my Solitude is sublime. . . . The roaring of the wind is my wife and the stars through the window pane are my Children.

If the echo is there, then so must

> Oft have I marked him, at some leisure hour,
> Stretched on the grass, or seated in the shade
> (Book VII, 782–83)

be the source of, in the "Ode to Autumn,"

> Who hath not seen thee oft amid thy Store?
> Sometimes whoever seeks abroad may find
> Thee sitting careless on a grassy floor . . . .

Unlike Francis Jeffrey, Keats had not been so put off by the protracted chunterings of *The Excursion* as to pass over either the beauty, or the deep residue of pain and bereavement, with which its discursive syntax is suffused. The truth is, however, that Keats had better reason than Jeffrey to be put off by Wordsworth's politics. The growing sense of crisis, in the summer of 1819, had led Keats to write, in "The Fall of Hyperion":

> "None can usurp this height . . .
> But those to whom the miseries of the world
> Are misery, and will not let them rest.
> All else who find a haven in the world,

Where they may thoughtless sleep away their days,
If by a chance into this fane they come,
Rot on the pavement where thou rotted'st half."

A few weeks afterward, he wrote in a letter, "I hope sincerely I shall be able to put a Mite of help to the Liberal side of the Question before I die"—perhaps as a political journalist. That same sense of crisis had aroused very different sentiments in Wordsworth himself.

> There has been [he had written in April, 1817] a general out-cry among sensible people in this neighbourhood against the remissness of Government in permitting the free circulation of injurious writings. . . . A Revolution will, I think, be staved off for the present, nor do I even apprehend that the disposition to rebellion may not without difficulty be suppressed. . . .

It is painful to come upon that word *suppressed* in light of what was to occur on August 16, 1819, when a gathering at St. Peter's Fields in Manchester in support of parliamentary reform ended, after troops were called in, with what has been known ever since as the Massacre of Peterloo. However appalling he found that event, by then Wordsworth's attitudes had hardened. He had once witnessed "human nature seeming born again," and then lived to acknowledge that it had not changed. His reaction may be deplored, but the record is worth looking at. Wordsworth in 1990 has been there before us.

T. S. Eliot in 1988

On the fifteenth of November, 1918, T. S. Eliot paid a visit to the Hogarth Press, which would later publish *The Waste Land*. "A polished, cultivated, elaborate young American," was the way Virginia Woolf described him in her diary for that day. They would become and remain friends. Even so, there was a temperamental difference that kept them wary of one another's work. We find her writing: "I taxed him with wilfully concealing his transitions. He said that explanation was unnecessary. If you put it in, you dilute the facts. You should feel these without explanation." In that same entry she went on to note: "He cant read Wordsworth when Wordsworth deals with nature."

Well, of course. A thirty-year-old expatriate dandy from St. Louis is not likely to have had much affinity with the great gray ruminant of Grasmere. By the 1930s he would have amended this to some degree, admitting that he enjoyed Wordsworth's poetry now "as I cannot enjoy Shelley's"—enjoyed it more than when he'd first read it. He's not alone in this. But for Virginia Woolf the affinity with the nineteenth century was always there. She would complain, sometime after *The Hollow Men* came out, that "for our sins we have only a few pipers on hedges like Yeats and Tom Eliot, de la Mare— exquisite frail twittering voices one has to hollow one's hand to hear, whereas old Wth fills the room." She loved *The Prelude*, and in the diary entries for her later years the name of Wordsworth keeps recurring, until you realize how much they have

Originally published as "T. S. Eliot's 'Different Voices' " in the *Yale Review* (Winter 1989).

in common: her "moments of being" are his "spots of time," alike in their visionary aura and their intense particularity. Virginia Woolf's later diaries are studded with entries like this:

> Cows feeding. The elm tree sprinkling its little leaves against the sky. Our pear tree swagged with pears. . . . Last night a great heavy plunge of bomb under the window. So near we both started. . . .

And here is the young Wordsworth in Paris, under circumstances not dissimilar, the lumbering syntax similarly charged:

> But that night
> When on my bed I lay, I was most moved
> And felt most deeply in what world I was;
> My room was high and lonely, near the roof
> Of a large Mansion or Hotel, a spot
> That would have pleased me more in other times,
> Nor was it wholly without pleasure then.
> With unextinguished taper I kept watch,
> Resting at intervals. The fear gone by
> Pressed on me almost like a fear to come.
> I thought of those September Massacres,
> Divided from me by a little month . . . .

And here is Eliot's account, in "Little Gidding," of his own experience of wartime:

> After the dark dove with the flickering tongue
> Had passed below the horizon of his homing
> While the dead leaves still rattled like tin
> Over the asphalt where no other sound was
> Between three districts where the smoke rose
> I met one walking, loitering and hurried
> As if blown toward me like the metal leaves
> Before the dawn wind unresisting. . . .

The lineage of those dead leaves on the asphalt, back through the *Inferno* to the sixth book of the *Aeneid* and the eleventh book of the *Odyssey,* is the region, I think one can say, in which

Eliot—a perpetual exile, as Frank Kermode has called him—
was most at home. He gave memory its poetic due; but he
never kept a diary, and when it came to autobiography he was,
of course, devious in the extreme. In any event, what con-
cerns me here is something more than a difference of individ-
ual temperament. It is rather the gulf, the rent that opened,
between Wordsworth's time and our own, in the texture of
English poetry.

Concerning that gulf, that rent, nobody has been more
eloquent than Virginia Woolf herself. At the beginning of *A
Room of One's Own* she finds herself recalling some familiar
lines of Tennyson and Christina Rossetti; wonders "if honestly
one could name two living poets" to compare with them; and
concludes that any such comparison is impossible. The living
poets, she observes with the clearheaded sympathy that makes
her prose so endlessly rewarding,

> express a feeling that is actually being made and torn out of us
> at the moment. One does not recognize it in the first place;
> often for some reason one fears it; one watches it with keen-
> ness and compares it jealously and suspiciously with the old
> feeling that one knew. Hence the difficulty of modern poetry;
> and it is because of this difficulty that one cannot remember
> more than two consecutive lines of any good modern poet.

The essay I've quoted from dates to October, 1928. What
Virginia Woolf described then as modern is still Modern, with
a capital M, in the same way that the New Criticism goes on
being New with a capital N. T. S. Eliot, as a chief instigator of
the first (if not of both—and his objections to the second are
at least strenuous enough to give one pause), stands for some-
thing. He casts a shadow. Perhaps his later eminence as a man
of letters has something to do with this, but I've tended to
forget all about him when it came to the naming of influences.
And yet it may be that no single poem written in this century
has had more influence than *The Waste Land*. It may or may
not turn out to be his most enduring work; but in the sense of
having occasioned a gulf, a rending, a before and after, I see it
as Eliot's masterpiece.

The late Richard Ellmann referred to *The Waste Land* as his ode to dejection. Whether Eliot would have been pleased by the comparison, one can't be sure. Toward Coleridge as a critic he was respectful; he found *Kubla Khan* deplorable, but he spoke of *Dejection: An Ode* as "one piece of [Coleridge's] formal verse which in its passionate self-revelation rises almost to the height of great poetry." What Eliot couldn't have known, but what makes comparison unavoidable, once you've thought about it, is that an early draft of this same ode was going to turn up—a draft which Coleridge himself, as his own severest critic, had pruned down in much the same way Pound did the manuscript of *The Waste Land*. Coleridge's original draft ran to something like 450 rambling and self-indulgent lines—just a bit longer than the scaled-down *Waste Land*, but all of three times as long as the version Coleridge eventually published. As with *The Waste Land*, its occasion seems to have been the panic of experiencing (to use the glum clinical term) a loss of affect:

> A grief without a pang, void, dark and drear,
> A stifled, drowsy, unimpassioned grief . . . .

The resolution is much the same. Both poems give the last word, so to speak, to the forces of nature. For Coleridge, it's the howling of a Lake Country gale; for Eliot, it's

>   a damp gust
> Bringing rain . . .
>
> The jungle crouched, humped in silence
> Then spoke the thunder
> DA . . . .

Where the two of them do part company is in the resources of language they draw upon. Coleridge, however up-to-date his neurosis, speaks throughout in the ranting vocatives of a diction nobody can now go back to—cannot go back, if Virginia Woolf is correct, because the way we perceive what we feel has been altered.

Walk along the corridor of any hospital, or along almost

any city thoroughfare, and you overhear people talking—not to themselves, as one might once have put it, but to a succession of unseen interlocutors. It is of such interior exchanges, we now discover, that our mental life is all too frequently composed. Far from functioning as autonomous units, we are more like the scrambled segments of an enormous psychic jigsaw puzzle. Pound put it more elegantly in his "Portrait d'une Femme":

> No! there is nothing! In the whole and all,
> Nothing that's quite your own.
> Yet this is you.

It was T. S. Eliot more than any other, if I'm not mistaken, who showed us the means of rendering this altered texture— who, one might say, first mapped the territory, if a map could be envisioned that combined the edginess of a chessboard with the random shifts of a kaleidoscope and the awful precision of a seismograph.

The title of the poem I'm making all these claims for—as the facsimile edition revealed—was originally to have been *He Do the Police in Different Voices.* In a lecture given as late as 1953, entitled "The Three Voices of Poetry," Eliot would say, or seem to be saying, that it wasn't until 1938 that overheard voices began to urge themselves on him. This can't be literally true; but anyhow he then cited Mrs. Cluppins, in the case of *Bardell v. Pickwick,* testifying that "the voices was very loud, sir, and forced themselves upon my ears." Well, back in 1921, when he typed the manuscript we now have in facsimile, for the title he later crossed out Eliot likewise drew on the work of Dickens. Midway through *Our Mutual Friend,* Mrs. Betty Higdon, the prototype of so many intrepid female vagrants, in better times is describing the "very long boy" to whom she has given employment: "You mightn't think it, but Sloppy is a beautiful reader of a newspaper. He do the Police in different voices."

So, displacing the bard's single, self-revealing voice, in *The Waste Land* we have the ventriloqual Sloppy of an entire culture: its longwinded nattering, its frozen standoffs and suppressed rejoinders, its dredged-up snatches of remembered diction with the connectives worn away; the voices seeping in unidentified, random, expressive of—well, of precisely what, a generation of interpreters has been trying to spell out, and we still don't know. New items do keep coming to one's notice. I've just lately found something M. L. Rosenthal wrote about the lines near the end of "The Burial of the Dead":

That corpse you planted last year in your garden—
Has it begun to sprout? Will it bloom this year?

That corpse, he says, "is the great corpse of all the war dead." I find this so very moving that I feel it must be right—though who knows? Thinking of it, anyhow, gives an added pathos to one more pawn in an excruciatingly sprawled-out game of chess: Albert, the husband who's just been demobilized, back after four years in the army and wanting a good time—what is he but one of the uncountable number of lesser casualties that go to make up our altered consciousness of the world we live in? Reading how at his job with Lloyd's Bank, Eliot had found himself busy "trying to elucidate knotty points in that appalling document the Peace Treaty," I couldn't help seeing that experience as one more interwoven component. But if it's there in fact, it isn't insisted on. Nothing is, in this strangely muted collage—this *bricolage,* as some critics have called it—of hitherto unconnected voices, which has exerted such power over us. As a result of that lack of insistence—or so it seems to me—an entire generation of poetic arbiters took it as their function to insist on our not insisting. Their descendants and disciples are still far from outnumbered—which makes it the more bemusing to find Eliot himself, in one of his periodic reconsiderations, attesting to "a certain merit in melodious raving, which can be a genuine contribution to literature, when it responds effectually to that permanent appetite of humanity for an occasional feast of drums and cymbals."

There were always rebel upstarts, of course. Think of Allen Ginsberg. He's in the anthologies now, but for a good while one had the impression that he was, well, *audible,* but somehow, and possibly for that very reason, not quite a poet. I mean, all that raving, that self-revelation. Hadn't those gone out with Coleridge and his vocatives:

> O Lady! in this wan and heartless mood,
> To other thoughts by yonder throstle woo'd,

and so on? Only there was Eliot himself addressing a Lady— addressing the Deity even, and appearing to mean it personally. There he was—according to his own words, a few years after the fact—not simply addressing but haranguing an audience. Was he entitled? Certain arbiters thought not: such was the force of the notion of poetic decorum that had taken hold, and that was (if I am correct) preeminently his doing, however unintended. From the diffidence of J. Alfred Prufrock he had come round unmistakably to wanting, like old Wordsworth, to fill a room. Could he do it? Could it be done? Or are we all condemned to go on twittering in the hedges, hoping somebody will be kind enough to pause and listen? I think we still don't know.

John Donne

More than half a century has passed since T. S. Eliot wrote, at the tercentenary of the death of John Donne, "We probably understand sympathetically Donne to-day better than poets and critics fifty years hence will understand him." If the phrasing sounds uncomfortable, it's no wonder. Not quite twenty years before, Eliot had made some pronouncements that are still quoted, and that had much to do with the recent high repute of Donne, among others of his time. In 1926 Eliot had given some lectures on Donne, but chose not to turn them into a book. By 1931, the tercentenary year, he was clearly in the process of backing off. His initial fervor—"A thought to Donne was an experience; it modified his sensibility. When a poet's mind is perfectly equipped for its work, it is constantly amalgamating disparate experiences"—had evaporated; now he was saying that in Donne, "learning is just information suffused with emotion, or combined with emotion not essentially relevant to it." Behind the squinting contortion of that forecast was no boast of superior sympathy but the squirm of embarrassment: times change, and thinking falls all over itself.

Such thinking, however evanescent, is the stuff of literary reputation. Milton and Wordsworth have had their undoubted, if less febrile, ups and downs. In the early 1940s the poems of Donne were still very much in fashion, and I myself absorbed what Helen Gardner saw in retrospect as the pervasive notion that "Donne was a more interesting and significant poet than

Milton." (F. O. Matthiessen, in *The Achievement of T. S. Eliot,* at least implied it.) But the pervasiveness of that notion may say more about a generation's vendetta against epic size than about Donne himself. Milton is no longer execrated; Wordsworth has come very near to being trendy; any day now, epic sublimity in English may be approached with something other than an involuntary sigh.

And what of Donne, half a century after Eliot's own second thoughts? If he is no longer trendy, neither has he been relegated anywhere—even though in the latest major study, *John Donne: Life, Mind and Art* (Oxford, 1981), John Carey does hint at a continuing urge to cut back on the favorable notices. At any rate, Donne is still, as he always has been, controversial—one of those poets toward whose work a sigh or a shrug is barely conceivable. I have read that Borges singled out the lines

> License my roving hands, and let them go
> Before, behind, between, above, below.
> O my America! my new-found land,

from Donne's elegy "To His Mistress Going to Bed," as a demonstration of his greatness as a poet. C. S. Lewis, no partisan, described it as proof that Donne was a sadist—a conclusion disputed at length by William Empson, on the basis of his reading of a single line; and since there is no way to know which of several variants Donne would finally have preferred, a resolution is unlikely.

Even when Donne's text is not in dispute, both meaning and estimate remain unsettled. Concerning one of the most frequently reprinted of all his poems, "The Ecstasy," the wrangling has been long, vehement, and similarly inconclusive. Coleridge praised it, and so did Pound. For C. S. Lewis, it was arguably a "much nastier" poem than the bedtime elegy. What Donne himself had in mind—seduction by way of Neoplatonic sophistries, or something rather more elevated—would seem by now almost, if not entirely, irretrievable. There is the vocabulary to be dealt with: not only an alchemical term such as *concoction,* but the title word itself is to be approached with caution. When Keats wrote of the nightingale *pouring its soul abroad* "in such an ecstasy," he was using the word with more precision than we generally do. These days, as all currencies are debased, the worst ravages are linguistic—and so we need to be reminded that etymologically an ecstasy is a going forth (*ek-stasis*) and further that in the vocabulary of the Neoplatonists it denoted the going forth of the soul to be united with the object of its desire. Clearly this, and not some more generalized rapture, is Donne's subject; but how much nearer it brings us to the poet's own frame of mind, I am not sure.

Possibly a greater stumbling block than *ecstasy*, a word Donne used rarely, is *soul*—which he mentions so habitually as to be troubling for a twentieth-century reader. Whatever philosophical uncertainties the poet may have been prey to, for him there was no doubt that the soul existed, as genuinely as the corporeal frame itself. He also believed that the sun revolved about the earth—believed it, notwithstanding the Copernican heresy, to which he not infrequently referred, in much the same way that he believed in a Deity with power over the human soul. He troubled himself a good deal over theology, as only a believer with an excitable intellect would be inclined to do. It is partly because of this excitability that people discovering Donne for the first time tend to view him as an old poet with surprisingly modern attitudes. Though of late a considerable edifice of critical writing has been built on such misreading, I can't suppose that any of those engaged in the construction (and deconstruction) would say that outright misreading is therefore to be encouraged. And in any event the stumbling block remains: John Donne wrote of the soul as an entity whose existence he did not doubt. This should be clear from the first poem of his ever to appear in print—"The Expiration," published in 1609 in a volume of Airs, with a musical setting by Ferrabosco. "So, so," it begins, "break off this last lamenting kiss, / Which sucks two souls, and vapours both away. . . ."

Donne's friend and exact contemporary Ben Jonson, who in the familiar lyric beginning "Drink to me only with thine eyes," declared that

> The thirst that from the soul doth rise
> Doth ask a drink divine,

likewise equated the soul with breathing: the wreath of roses which his lady had declined to accept, but only sniffed at and sent back again, is declared by the singer to grow and smell "not of itself, but thee." Hyperbole of this sort was rampant at the time, and is of course typical of Donne. An earlier line in the song—"But might I of Jove's nectar sup, / I would not change for thine"—does, however, suggest a difference between the two poets. The names of Venus, of Mercury, even of Jove, appear now and then in the poems of Donne, but not nearly so often as do saints, heretics, canonizations and other ecclesiastical paraphernalia; and when Love is personified, it is more likely to be in such terms as "Love, any devil else but you." Unlike Jonson, whose frame of mind may be described as classical, Donne at his most profane is essentially a Christian poet.

He was born in 1572, into a time when theological and political turmoil were even more thornily intertwined than they now are. That same year witnessed the slaughter of French Protestants on the eve of St. Bartholomew, when Donne was only a few months old. The air of Elizabethan England was poisoned by fear of popery; Donne's parents were Catholic; his brother Henry was sent to prison for harboring a Roman priest, and died there. John Donne himself studied at Oxford, and later at Cambridge, but without then taking a degree since to do so meant subscribing to the Thirty-Nine Articles and adhering to the Church of England. The year he was twenty, he was admitted to Lincoln's Inn for the study of law. He appeared around this time as a wit and a worldling, "attentive to ladies and a great frequenter of plays." He must also by then have begun writing verse, which—as was the fashion among young men of that station—circulated in manuscript, but which he disdained to publish. Among the earliest of these poems were probably the satires, whose prevailing note is sounded by the opening lines of Satire 2:

> Sir; though (I thank God for it) I do hate
> Perfectly all this town. . . .

What caused his gorge to rise is a bad poet who is also a lawyer—the stereotypical creep, still revoltingly alive and identifiable notwithstanding the Elizabethan attire. That the author is himself a poet and a lawyer only adds to the scathing force of the indictment. At once angry and ambitious, he already knows all about the world:

> Bastardy abounds not in king's titles, nor
> Simony and sodomy in churchmen's lives,
> As these things do in him; by these he thrives.

At his most forthright, Donne is anything but simple. The text of this satire contains, along with a spate of legalistic expressions, a liberal seasoning of religious ones: papists, confessors, Schoolmen, canonists, abbeys, Pater nosters and litanies, Carthusian fasts, the Church Fathers, Luther, even Satan himself are all at hand. What is here implicit, the third Satire makes explicit: a protracted wrestling within himself concerning "our mistress true religion"—or more precisely, the rival claims of the various sects and their spokesmen, clerical or otherwise:

> Fool and wretch, wilt thou let thy soul be tied
> To man's laws, by which she shall not be tried
> At the last day? Or will it then boot thee
> To say a Philip, or a Gregory,
> A Harry, or a Martin taught thee this?

More than twenty years were to pass before the conflict in his own mind was finally, or anyhow ostensibly, resolved, and Donne made his reluctant entrance into a career in the Church of England. The reluctance was not entirely doctrinal; for all his cynicism about preferments and favorites and hangers-on at Whitehall, a life at Court, or in diplomacy, was what he had aimed for. In fact, such a career would seem to have been assured; after taking part in two naval expeditions against Spain—to Cadiz in 1596 and to the Azores in the following year—he had become secretary to Sir Thomas Egerton, the Lord Keeper and an ally of the Earl of Essex. Before long Essex would have angered the Queen, turned against her and been sent to the Tower. He was executed in 1601; but John Donne's own lost prospects had nothing to do with the fortunes of any royal favorite.

Concerning his love affair with his employer's niece, Ann More, their secret marriage, and his dismissal and temporary imprisonment on the charge of violating canon law, we have the facts but hardly any of the flavor, except whatever may incidentally have been preserved in the poems of Donne. The effort to sort out which of these were addressed to his wife, and to just what in their life together they refer, remains inconclusive. Donne was twenty-nine, his wife barely sixteen, at the time of their marriage. They lived isolated, dependent on relatives, friends, and literary patrons, in a damp little house at Mitcham in Surrey, where year by year another child arrived, until improving prospects made it possible for them to move to London. There, still in her early thirties, Ann Donne gave birth for the twelfth time. The baby was born dead, and Ann herself died soon after. Whatever else may be said of it, the marriage must often have been overhung with gloom; and if it is assumed that such poems as "Twicknam Garden" and "A Nocturnal Upon St. Lucy's Day" were written during the years at Mitcham, their funereal tone is understandable. It is now believed that the Holy Sonnets also date, at least mainly, to this stage of Donne's life, and not to a later one.

By degrees, at any rate, Donne came into favor with the court of James I, and from 1621 onward the sometime rake and libertine was known not as Jack but as Dr. Donne, Dean of St. Paul's, and was famed for his preaching. The funerary effigy for which he posed dressed in his shroud is still to be seen, the only monument to survive the destruction of the old St. Paul's in the fire of 1666. Donne's last sermon was delivered there a month before he died, and according to Izaak Walton, his earliest biographer, many among those who "heard his faint and hollow voice" were conscious "that Dr. Donne *had preached his own funeral sermon.*" In it, as he lingered over "the *periods* and *transitions* in this life," he recalled his wife's own passage, fourteen years before: "In the wombe, the dead *child* kills the *Mother* that conceived it"; and later, "The *wombe* which should be the *house of life* becomes *death* it selfe, if *God* leave us there."

In thus harping on the paradoxes of mortality, the writing of Donne is all of a piece—and of a piece as well with *Hamlet*'s gravediggers and the *Urn Burial* of Sir Thomas Browne. Theirs was a time when outbreaks of plague were frequent, and when hitherto forbidden anatomical studies were soon to disclose the workings of the heart as an actual, physiological pump. From the beginning, Donne's poems are dense with allusions to the "*corruption* and *putrefaction vermiculation* and *incineration*, and dispersion in and from the grave" that were to be the running theme of his sermons: not only carcasses and dissections, gout, fever, dropsy, powder burns, waking in a "cold quicksilver sweat," but colds and even flea bites. It has been said that the poetry of Donne is not sensuous—a strange commentary, it seems to me, on work so stunningly (and indeed at times revoltingly) physical. This quality was, I think, mainly why it interested me at a time when Wordsworth's didn't, or not very much. Even so patently formulaic and conventional a lyric as "The Bait," for me, leaped off the page and ran along the nerves:

> Let others freeze with angling reeds,
> And cut their legs, with shells and weeds,
> Or treacherously poor fish beset,
> With strangling snare, or windowy net;
>
> Let coarse bold hands, from slimy nest
> The bedded fish in banks out-wrest. . . .

With all the brooding on mortality, and linked to it by some organic tissue, Donne had what Marianne Moore called gusto. He was interested in things. At his most self-centered—the accusation keeps being made, as though the self could be otherwise—he reaches out in all directions and to great distances: even on a voluptuous morning after, as he upbraids the sun for meddling, his imagination is global:

> Look, and tomorrow late, tell me
> Whether both th'Indias of spice and mine
> Be where thou left'st them, or lie here with me.

The original circumnavigation of the globe had been completed just half a century before Donne was born, and so vivid was his consciousness of it, of the fact that the world is round, contending as it did with the old geography, all those maps depicting the corners of the world, that the names of remote places seem to throng in wait, pressing for any mention however farfetched. In this Donne is like Emily Dickinson, who is sometimes linked with him on other grounds. Both speak of Tenerife, which neither had ever seen—though Donne himself traveled in its general direction when he sailed against Spain—but whose imagined altitude gave a value to the name itself. And so it becomes possible to connect the familiar lines from the second of the *Anniversaries,*

> Thou look'st through spectacles; small things seem great
> Below; but up unto the watch-tower get
> And see all things despoiled of fallacies . . .

with the cupola at Amherst, the seat of Emily Dickinson's uniquely incandescent vision of the world.

From his own watch-tower, Donne had a vision otherwise quite different. For Emily Dickinson, the world seen from that cupola on Main Street was somehow "new every morning." All those voyages to the New World notwithstanding, for Donne the world was *old*—was, as many seriously believed it to be, near the appointed end. Becalmed at Mitcham, he had written, as he did every Tuesday, to Sir Henry Goodyer—the closest of all his friends, and he had many—of the world out there as "a garment made of remnants, a life raveled out into ends, a line discontinued." That it gave him pleasure to think of the world in rags is, in the circumstances, hardly surprising. (He would caution himself presently against such ill-wishing.) At any rate, the notion of a thing in rags recurs through the poems: the rags of religion, in the third Satire; the worn-out tufftaffaty worn by the purveyor of scandals at Court, in the fourth; the rotting sails of "The Storm"; in "The Broken Heart," that organ itself as a thing of rags; and in "Good Friday, 1613. Riding Westward,"

> that flesh which was worn,
> By God, for his apparel, ragged, and torn?

The world in rags, as "but a carcase," as a ghost, as a dry cinder is the obsessive central theme of *The Anniversaries,* brought forth from the gloom and damp of Mitcham—whose two installments together constitute by far the longest (and in some ways the gloomiest) poem Donne ever wrote. It is—the more since it is a work Donne chose to publish, in 1611 and 1612—once again controversial. A masterpiece, or a maundering and outlandish occasional poem? Just possibly it is both. The occasion, as the title makes explicit, is "the untimely death of Mistress Elizabeth Drury"—a girl of fifteen, whom Donne never met, and to whose father, Sir Robert Drury, he hoped to recommend himself. Since "the frailty and decay of this whole world" are seen, for the purposes of the work in hand, to issue from her demise, there is a certain ricketyness about the project. Ben Jonson found it blasphemous. Marjorie Hope Nicolson thought it might be rescued if it were seen as a late-blooming elegy for another Elizabeth, the Virgin Queen who had died eight years before. But that hardly seems possible, since Donne made what he was doing quite explicit. He originally planned to go on producing an installment a year, as each new anniversary came round. But in 1612 (thanks to Sir Robert Drury, as it must be noted) his fortunes improved, he moved from Mitcham to London, and from then on there would have been less time anyhow. As it is, the poem runs on rather like an orator entangled in his own peroration. Readers of anthologies know it mainly by way of a purple patch or two, which do not begin to suggest the cumulative force of the refrain:

> She, she is dead; she's dead; when thou know'st this,
> Thou know'st how poor a trifling thing man is

through the culminating variant:

> She, she is gone; she is gone; when thou know'st this,
> What fragmentary rubbish this world is
> Thou know'st, and that it is not worth a thought. . . .

All this is of course hyperbole, not literal assertion. What gives so unwieldy a production its surprising power is, I think, that Donne in fact cared a good deal about a world that is, after nearly four centuries, still recognizable:

> 'Tis all in pieces, all coherence gone;
> All just supply, and all relation:
> Prince, subject, father, son, are things forgot,
> For every man alone thinks he hath got
> To be a phoenix, and that then can be
> None of that kind, of which he is, but he.

When Yeats wrote of how things fall apart, was he borrowing, even subconsciously? Or did he simply see the same thing happening all over again? In either event, not much in the poems of Donne is so likely to bring Yeats to mind. A more plausible successor would be Marianne Moore, for whom a paramount concern was with naturalness—with clearing away all the limp, pat, dreary, stilted locutions that inspired her dislike of Poetry with a capital P. The vivacity, the abrupt music, the occasional cacophony of the speaking voice: it is for these that the poems of Donne continue to be read. Eliot thought so—continued to think so even as he voiced his second thoughts: "It is hardly too much to say that Donne enlarged the possibilities of lyric verse as no other English poet has done."

This he did by making the lyric also dramatic. The cry of the girl in the "Elegy on His Mistress"—"oh, oh / Nurse, O my love is slain, I saw him go / O'er the white Alps alone"—has the ring of a speech from a play by Shakespeare. Donne was ventriloquist enough to have ventured more than one poem entirely in the voice of a woman: "Break of Day," "Confined Love," and the verse epistle "Sappho to Philaenis"—a piece Helen Gardner preferred to believe Donne could not have written, though John Carey allows it to stand, calling it "the first homosexual love poem in English"—are to be read so. Elsewhere, the brisk syncopations of direct address roughen the surface of poems otherwise conventional. In "The Expiration," which I take to be early, the imperative becomes an enjambed leap from one stanza to the next:

> We asked none leave to love; nor will we owe
> Any, so cheap a death, as saying, Go;
>
> Go. . . .

More characteristic, and probably later (as I believe; but no one knows) is the way he can make anyone in the world his own interlocutor: "For God's sake, hold your tongue, and let me love."

More typical still is the speaker addressing his own soul: "What if this present were the world's last night?" This is the habitual mode of the sermons as well as of the religious lyrics:

> Who sees God's face, that is self life, must die.
> What a death were it then to see God die?
> It made his own lieutenant Nature shrink,
> It made his footstool crack, and the sun wink.
> Could I behold those hands which span the poles,
> And turn all spheres at once, pierced with those holes?

Lines such as these have an intensity the love poems nowhere quite equal. The extremes of a baroque sensibility are to be found throughout the works of Donne. But those extremes, the paradox, the hyperbole, here transcend their literary function to become a way of apprehending the stress of being— reality as a process, a condition to be entered rather than observed. Many readers, and I am one, have found it more confusing than helpful to refer to a metaphysical school of poets, the term having long ago become a catchall for whatever is merely ingenious, elaborate, or farfetched. But the greatest of Donne's religious poetry is metaphysical in the root sense of going beyond rational exploration. The "physics" of the early seventeenth century, with its persistent imagery of turning spheres, of macro- and microcosms, of hierarchy and degree, has been superseded. Yet the continuity of the human imagination is such that along with the speaking voice, the profane and sweaty ardor, the force of what John Donne most deeply believed is with us still.

Marianne Moore

Asked once whether she regarded herself as part of the American tradition, Marianne Moore responded by calling herself "an American chameleon on an American leaf."

This could have been one of her jokes—an escape hatch, a self-protective disappearing act such as her poems not infrequently constitute. Of a piece with "To a Chameleon," which begins (and the first word is clearly no accident), "Hid by the August foliage and fruit of the grapevine," and with her famous wish

> . . . to be a dragon,
> a symbol of the power of Heaven—of silkworm
> size or immense; at times invisible

is the reticence she admired. It was her dictum, offered more than once, "when obscurity was deplored, [that] one should be as clear as one's natural reticence allows one to be." And notwithstanding what she called "a burning desire to be explicit," her own natural reticence was very great.

So, although the prose pieces collected by Patricia C. Willis in *The Complete Prose of Marianne Moore* (Elizabeth Sifton/ Viking, 1986) do shed light on what went into her poems and how it got there, we learn very little from them of those inner recesses, those reserves of feeling, concerning which the po-

---

Adapted from a review originally published in the *Boston Sunday Globe* and from a paper originally read at the Chicago Public Library Cultural Center on May 20, 1986, later published as "The Matter and the Manner" in the *Cream City Review* (Summer 1988).

ems are not explicit. That those reserves did exist may be inferred from such observations as that her favorite poem was the Book of Job; or from an essay called "The Knife," published originally in *House and Garden,* which purports to be no more than a connoisseur's appreciation of several well-turned implements—an ebony-handled kitchen blade, a paper knife, an Etruscan sword—but which then moves on to consider the arts of the stonecutter, and concludes with the Confucian maxim (quoted elsewhere in the volume, not once but several times over) that "If there is a knife of resentment in the heart, the mind fails to act with precision."

Perhaps, even here, the precision is the important thing: it is, after all, inseparable from the discipline indispensable to any art. "Aesthetic rigor," she called it, mildly deploring its absence from the work of Vachel Lindsay. She quoted, with implicit approval, Anna Pavlova on the "merciless discipline" of the School of the Imperial Ballet. The discipline of the ballet barre—and that Marianne Moore should feel an affinity for it is only momentarily surprising—is meaningless until and unless it has become a matter of *self*-discipline. The degree to which Miss Moore was a creature of self-discipline is engagingly revealed by her confession that "sometimes in the past" she hadn't eaten breakfast "until about noon, I was so determined to get my mail answered. Now I eat as soon as I get up—cereal, fruit juice. If there is a really urgent letter, I answer it first. Someone may be in a hurry for a book for Christmas and wants it signed."

A Puritanism so frankly obliging must by now be almost extinct—which is not to say that the more rankling and troublesome forms of it have ceased to operate. Nor is it to say that Miss Moore herself never moralized. In her prose as in her verse, she could do so quite explicitly, as when she wrote of Hollywood—a place that, she begins deliciously by observing, "has the bad luck to be outstarred by its whereabouts: eucalyptus-trees, calico horses with pale eyes, bits of sea with cormorants or pelicans, or rolling hills with shadows. George Arliss is neutralized by the dogville-comedy aspect of his support and Greta Garbo is shabbied by luxury. Plucked eyebrows, reinforced eyelashes, a slouch do not improve an already fortunate equipment." A few pages further on, in a review of the art film "Lot in Sodom," the rigor intensifies: "As you know better than anyone else does, how to open your combination safe, a civilization that has reached an extreme of culture, is going to have pleasure, will have it and is meting out justice to any man that interferes. But pleasure is not joy, it is strangling horror—the serpent that thrust forward rigid—and does not know it ever was anything else."

But so unqualified a tone is exceptional. More typical—of her prose as of her poetry—are the modulations of simple delight through aesthetic rumination and ethical unease, as in her account of the circus: "The gilded wagons and bellows-warbled, now high, now low, hollow music of the circus have again invited us to wander among the cages. Toulouse-Lautrec's, Seurat's, and Emanuel Fay's equestriennes . . . Picasso's saltimbanques and harlequins, assert by implication that they have not been based on nothing. . . . Rashness and regality may not be teaching us anything; animals should not be taken from their proper surroundings, and in staging an act the bad taste of patrons should not be deferred to; but apparently this medicinally mingled feast of sweet and bitter is not poisonous; it is not all aconite."

Elsewhere—particularly in the book reviews that over the years made up no small part of her livelihood—the pleasure is unequivocal. Gusto is one of her favorite words; and surely no Puritan ever had more of it. In 1967, having passed her eightieth year, she exclaims over a recent trip abroad: "Have you been to Greece, seen the olive trees and the goats, and the magpies flitting and hopping?" She praises Robert Frost for having "raised naturalness to an art." She lauds "the riot of gorgeousness in which the imagination of Wallace Stevens takes refuge." She singles out for notice the "intense particularity" of Thomas Hardy, citing a line as an example: "The rain clams her apron till it clings." Reviewing the letters of Emily Dickinson, she writes that "unless it is conceited for the hummingbird or the osprey to not behave like a chicken, one does not find her conceited." In raising an objection, she is almost (but not quite) always friendly, as when she observes of e.e. cummings that "a Saint Sebastian . . . may be hid by too many arrows of awareness."

Ezra Pound is important to her. Gertrude Stein is in an odd way a kindred spirit. That her famous admiration for the doings of athletes was total and unfeigned, her response to the queries of George Plimpton happily makes clear. What her collected prose makes clear above all, however, is the primacy of her admiration for Henry James. Her first published story shows his influence; and she was never more eloquent than in the tribute entitled "Henry James as a Characteristic American":

> Love is the thing more written about than anything else, and in the mistaken sense of greed. Henry James seems to have been haunted by awareness that rapacity destroys what it is successful in acquiring. He feels a need "to see the other side as well as his own, to feel what his adversary feels" . . . we have no scruple about insisting that he was American; not if the American is, as he thought, "intrinsically and actively ample`. . . reaching westward, southward, anywhere, everywhere," with a mind "incapable of the shut door in any direction."

Earlier in the same essay, Miss Moore speaks of the " 'almost indescribable naturalness' which disappears in the fancy writing of his imitators." "Naturalness" may seem an odd term to use of a writer so mannered. The same might be said of Marianne Moore herself. Her manner was her own; it did not come easily, and is the more to be treasured for the rigors that produced it.

That there were rigors, including periods of self-doubt, her position in later life as (to borrow the words of Charles Tomlinson) a kind of national *pet* may have tended to obscure. "One writes as one must and not as one should," she told a college student who had been puzzling over her most famous poem ("I, too, dislike it . . ."), "and . . . I have no deceived impression that my faults and short-comings, by some helpful legerdemain, partake of magic which is foreign to them." Her habitual self-protectiveness is no doubt at work here, but is there not also the weariness and resignation of one inured to lost causes? One hears a sigh: "I do not wonder that you find it difficult to see my lines entitled POETRY, as poetry. I regard my compositions as 'observations' whereas in poetry, I feel, one has the poetry and the form together, as something rapt and irrefutable."

For the student was not alone in being puzzled. As late as 1950, Marianne Moore was still not included in Brooks and Warren's *Understanding Poetry*, where such contemporaries as Eliot, Pound, and Stevens were well represented. For this omission the most likely explanation is that the strangeness and difficulty of her work had simply scared off the critics.

Certainly the difficulty is real enough. As nearly as I can recall, I first encountered the work of Marianne Moore in F. O. Matthiessen's selection for the *Oxford Book of American Verse*, published in 1950. What I found there was tough going, and remained so until very much later: as late, in fact, as the summer of 1978, during a stay in a rented house on the coast of Maine. That house had many attractions, a fairly straightforward enumeration of which found its way into a little poem of mine called "The Cove." Thus, in writing

> and when there's fog
> or a gale we get a fire going, listen
> to Mozart, read Marianne Moore

and so on, I was being perfectly literal: among those attractions was a copy of *The Marianne Moore Reader*, which I found on the shelves and proceeded to read with total absorption. What kept me reading was not so much a formal model as an opening up of possibilities. Elizabeth Hardwick, writing of Sylvia Plath, refers to a "preference for precision over rhetoric," adding that "perhaps this greed for particulars is the true mark of the poetry of women in our time." Whether or not this is generally true, precision and attention to detail are what Marianne Moore's work is all about. And that is what I found attractive: a clear and principled opposition to the dictum of Dr. Johnson that poetry ought not to "number the streaks on the tulip." This divergence becomes the more striking if one thinks of Robert Frost: for all the accuracy of observation that underlies a poem such as "Spring Pools" or "Blue Butterfly Day," the compact stanza form at which Frost excelled tends to mute or even suppress the particulars, rather than to elaborate them as Marianne Moore chose to do.

Not, of course, that she had any less interest in form: it could be argued—since she never borrowed a stanza pattern, even from herself, but invented a new one for each occasion—that she had more interest in poetic form than Frost did, or than most of us do. But in "An Octopus," her longest single poem, fidelity to subject matter becomes—literally, that subject being the glacial cover of Mount Rainier—paramount:

> Relentless accuracy is the nature of this octopus
> with its capacity for fact.
> "Creeping slowly as with meditated stealth,
> its arms seeming to approach from all directions,"
> it receives one under winds that "tear the snow to bits
> and hurl it like a sandblast
> shearing off twigs and loose bark from the trees."

Then comes a momentary shift into the poet's own voice:

> Is "tree" the word for these things
> "flat on the ground like vines"?
> some "bent in a half circle with branches on one side
> suggesting dust-brushes, not trees;
> some finding strength in union, forming little stunted groves
> their flattened mats of branches shrunk in trying to escape"
> from the hard mountain "planed by ice and polished by the
>   wind"—
> the white volcano with no weather side;
> the lightning flashing at its base,
> rain falling in the valleys, and snow falling on the peak—
> the glassy octopus symmetrically pointed,
> its claw cut by the avalanche
> "with a sound like the crack of a rifle,
> in a curtain of powdered snow launched like a waterfall."

And so the poem ends: though she did not borrow forms, Marianne Moore quoted contents at length and with abandon. That conclusion has something in common with "Novices"; but in its entirety "An Octopus" is unlike anything else of hers. It reminds me in some ways of—of all things—*The Prelude:* the same awed concern with natural violence, but above all the sense of intractability, the intractability of experience itself, with which Wordsworth wrestled long but which he never found a way of reducing to a manageable form. Embedded in what at first appears to be no more than a sprawling catchall of quotations and descriptive details are a number of precepts drawn (as the poet's own notes disclose) from none other than the Rules and Regulations of the U.S. Department of the Interior! Being myself by nature unruly, I take heart at seeing how a rigorist such as Marianne Moore could have fun with the very notion of rules—thus cheerfully defying the stricture of Yvor Winters (which seems to have struck such terror in the hearts of other critics, not to mention the poets they apply it to) against the Fallacy of Imitative Form. Coming upon that note to "An Octopus" made me laugh out loud. Marianne Moore is not only a strange poet; she is also, in her own sly and devious way, a very funny one.

Or so it seems to me. Look, for instance, at "The Hero"—originally the final section of what was then called "Part of a Novel, Part of a Poem, Part of a Play." I'm not at all sure I know what is going on in this poem; but whatever else there may be, I can't help seeing it as some kind of joke. There are owls in it, flying out

> on muffled wings, with twin yellow
> eyes—to and fro—
>
> with quavering water-whistle note, low,
>   high, in basso-falsetto chirps
>   until the skin creeps.

Well, we have this description of the owl and its call, but that call hasn't, so to speak, been *quoted* until, immediately following, we have

> Jacob when a-dying, asked
> Joseph: *Who* are these? [my italics]

How the poet got from the owl to the invocation of biblical patriarchs is totally inscrutable, it seems to me, without that *Who* . . . ?

And that's not all. A little further on, we find

> The decorous frock-coated Negro
> by the grotto

who—no, that one's not in the poem; it's my *who*, not Marianne Moore's—

> answers the fearless sightseeing hobo
> who asks the man she's with, what's this,
> what's that, where's Martha
> buried, "Gen-ral Washington
> there; his lady, here"; speaking
> as if in a play—not seeing her;

and so on. While I was trying to puzzle my way through this stanza, I circled "she" and wrote in the margin, "Who?"—and it wasn't until I'd made the connection between Jacob and the owl that it came to me, why, the very ambiguity over who *she* is (*can* the fearless sightseeing hobo—short, or so I'm told, for "homeless brother"—be female?), the ambiguity that made me write "Who?" in the margin, must be another of the poet's jokes. If anybody has a soberer explanation, I would love to hear it.

The hilarity to be found in our most respected authors tends, I suspect, to be underrated, or anyhow underpraised. Not long ago I reread *The Ambassadors,* for the third or fourth time—read it aloud, this time, with a friend, and discovered with some astonishment how much of it is downright funny. To connect Henry James with the jerboa, the pangolin, and all those amphibians and reptiles, might seem farfetched. But it isn't. In "An Octopus," the "sacrosanct remoteness" of the mountain peak is likened to none other than "Henry James 'damned by the public for decorum.' " That last set of quotation marks doesn't necessarily mean that the poet is quoting anyone other than herself, and if she is I don't know who (who?) it can be. The conclusion to the poem "New York," anyhow, turns out to be a modified quotation from James himself:

> not the plunder,
> but "accessibility to experience."

The coruscations of indirection and surprise of which the novels of James are protractedly, even maddeningly composed have their counterpart in a poem such as "The Mind Is an Enchanting Thing": those katydid-wing nettings and subdivisions, those dove-neck iridescences, that "conscientious inconsistency," down to the concluding negative: "it's / not a Herod's oath that cannot change." I would go so far as to suggest that the figure of the kiwi or apteryx, with its "rain-shawl / of haired feathers, . . . / feeling its way as though blind, / walking along with its eyes on the ground" could be describing at once the mind, attentive to the hidden byways of perception and response, and the somewhat bulky *person* of Henry James: a homage that is also a bit of a joke. I wouldn't put it past her.

But who knows? Much more *will* be known in due course, as those now engaged with Marianne Moore's notebooks and letters bring forth more of what they have discovered there. In the meantime, we have the author's categorical assertion, in what are offered as *The Complete Poems of Marianne Moore*, that "Omissions are not accidents." The most famous omission, just here, is of four and a half stanzas, or approximately nine-tenths, of the troublesomely titled "Poetry." One might surmise that when she cut it down to three lines, she did so as an act of rebellion. How many people who never read another word of hers know, or anyhow once read, that poem? I'll hazard a still worse conjecture: that an even greater number have been influenced by it, at that remove where any influence is almost certainly a bad one.

Over the past two or three years I've had occasion to read a considerable number of poems entered in various competitions; and I have noted with dismay, in verse otherwise free and unfettered, what feels like an epidemic rash of enjambments, as follows:

> how to pick up after themselves, to keep the apartment
> clean . . .

followed, on the same page, by

> the coats he never hangs on their
> hooks. . . .

Or, in another entry,

> The noise, the elbows, the crowded
> Subways. . . .

In the latter instance—and I could go on and on, I assure you—capitalizing the first word of the run-over line makes the effect all the more stiltedly arbitrary.

The persistence of this single mannerism cannot but cause one to wonder, sooner or later, where in the world it came from. For an answer—as well as a caution—I offer another look at "Poetry" in its original, untruncated version. It is written in syllabic verse, embodying one of those ad hoc stanza forms that were never repeated, with two pairs of rhyming lines and two other, nonrhyming ones: x a a b b y. Line by line, the syllabic count in the version published by the Egoist Press in 1921 is 19, 22, 11, 5, 8, 13. A later revision, which is to be found among the notes in the back of the 1981 edition of those so-called *Complete Poems*, discloses some fiddling with both rhyme and syllabic count. Besides the unmistakable deletion of an entire interjected sentence ("case after case / could be cited did / one wish it" from the third stanza, and a phrase—"in defiance of their opinion"—from the fifth and final one), it is instructive to come upon other, relatively inconspicuous changes. The original version of the poem opens:

> I, too, dislike it: there are things that are important beyond
>   all this fiddle.
> Reading it, however, with a perfect contempt for it, one dis-
>   covers that there is in
> it after all, a place for the genuine.

In the commonly reprinted later version, the second line has been pruned of a clause, "that there is," so as to indicate, as John Nims has observed, a preference for syntactical tightness over formal balance. (Of that balance, entailing a series of run-over lines, more in a moment.) A like afterthought shows itself in a tiny but instructive shift in the second stanza. Here is the original version: ". . . a / / high sounding interpretation that can be put upon them because they are / useful; when they become so derivative as to become unintelligible, the / same thing may be said for all of us—that we. . . ." In the revision, nothing is altered until the beginning of the second line: "useful. When they become so derivative as to become unintelligible, / the same thing may be said for all of us, that we. . . ."

Such fiddling with punctuation marks is of the sort that few poets, given the opportunity, can resist. But shifting "the" from the end of the second line to the beginning of the third—as though neither rhyme nor syllabic count, however carefully adhered to in the first place, finally mattered—must mean a more fundamental concern. I take that concern to be with naturalness, as opposed to the stale, the inane, the highfalutinly derivative—all reasons for disliking Poetry with a capital P.

It should now be clear that Marianne Moore wasn't wedded to her own idiosyncrasies—that she tended, rather, to be ambivalent about them. When one considers the abundance of formal idiosyncrasy here, one can more easily imagine what caused her to scuttle nine-tenths of the original in favor of

> I, too, dislike it.
>   Reading it, however, with a perfect contempt for it, one
>   discovers in
>   it, after all, a place for the genuine.

What she leaves us with is a little tune, keyed to a single vowel sound: not only is the monosyllabic pronoun "it" used four times over in a total of twenty-four words; but note how "*dis*like," "Read*ing*," "*with*," "per*fect*" (as usually pronounced), "*dis*covers," "*in*," and finally "genu*ine*," all echo that light central vowel. Thus given ear to, it becomes in effect a new poem, and one's delight in the artistry of Marianne Moore is reinforced. The one real idiosyncrasy remaining—that is, the enjambment of "one discovers in / it"—then becomes not high-handed but, within the aural scheme, inevitable: the dominant, the fulcrum of an audible structure. Likewise justifiable, if for reasons less subtle and more methodical, is the pattern of enjambments between the second and third lines of each of the succeeding stanzas. Here they are:

> high sounding interpretation can be put upon them but be-
> cause they are
> useful; when

in the second stanza;

> eat, elephants pushing, a wild horse taking a roll, a tireless
> wolf under
> a tree, and

in the third;

> school-books"; all these phenomena are important. One must
> make a distinction
> however; when

in the fourth; and in the fifth, the pivotal

> for inspection, "imaginary gardens with real toads in them,"
> shall we have
> it.

I hardly suppose that Marianne Moore intended anyone even to notice—much less spend the amount of time I've now spent on—what she was doing here. My guess is that she was simply amusing herself, playing a game whose rules were too ephemeral to be taken all that seriously. This having been said, a question arises: how many of those—some clearly no more than what she denigrated as half poets, but not necessarily all: I've seen not a few instances of what has become a kind of tic, in the work of people I genuinely admire, and I can't claim to be free of what I now regard as this defect myself—how many who have broken a line in such a manner, with no visible concern for either sound or syllabic count, would be able to name a source, an authority for doing so? How many ever actually read "Poetry"—read it, anyhow, with sufficient attention to be put on guard by its reference to half poets?

Depressing in its small way as this is, I'm aware it is nothing new. Hazlitt, in an unforgettable essay, provided a name for it: Vulgarity.

We live in a vulgar time and a vulgar country. Year by year the disease appears to spread, to become less treatable. Year by year, it seems more difficult to make oneself understood when one uses the term as Hazlitt, with cantankerous verve, labored to have it understood:

> Nothing is vulgar that is natural, spontaneous, unavoidable. Grossness is not vulgarity, ignorance is not vulgarity, awkwardness is not vulgarity: but all these become vulgar when they are affected and shewn off on the authority of others, or to fall in with *the fashion* or the company we keep. . . . The upper are not wiser than the lower orders, because they resolve to differ from them. The fashionable have the advantage of the unfashionable in nothing but the fashion.

In a free country, where theoretically everyone is an original, a member of no class or species, to have it hinted that one has inadvertently fallen in with the fashion, or the company one keeps, tends to bring on sweats of anxiety. "You're going to *hate* my line breaks," a poet said to me. *My* line breaks. Is to have been caught with one's hand in the cookie jar of affectation then so very heinous, embarrassing though it may be? In the nature of things, we are all susceptible to influence: it's the unconsidered literary trickle-down that causes us to squirm. Twice, I've been asked by a kindly editor, "Do you really want that echo of Yeats?" And of course I didn't—hadn't seen it was *there*. Something quite different is going on when May Swenson writes, very much in her own way, of the anhinga or the saguaro cactus; when Alfred Corn gives his somberly emblematic reading of the dogwood or the wild carrot; or when Brad Leithauser, in his stunning "Hesitancy," considers an ostrich at the Kyoto zoo; or when, more explicitly still, George Bradley launches his tribute to the Portuguese man-of-war with a gesture in the direction of Randall Jarrell: ". . . she sent postcards to only the nicer animals." Such unmistakable homages to one's forebears are not only proper but inevitable. Absolute originality would amount to dying of one's own poison, and I for one am not in favor of that.

But it's herd-following that I'm concerned with here. If the latest competitive entries I've seen are any indication, minimalism is finally on the wane. As the lines and the poems themselves grow longer, I've been sorry to observe a new monotony, a garrulously protracted mumble. What was once vertical is now horizontal, like those things "tree" is not the word for. As an influence, William Carlos Williams appears to have given way to the shadowy demesne of John Ashbery. The latter would be the first to see the irony here, having himself observed, "I think I'm famous among people who may never have read a line of my poetry." Those who *have* read more than a line now and then will know that notwithstanding a principled avoidance of definitive statement, he is no less capable than Marianne Moore of crisply meticulous detail. Given her lively interest in couture, she would have loved his account of Mania "dressed in the style of Joan Crawford in *Mildred Pierce,* in a severe suit with padded shoulders and a pillbox with a veil crowning the pincurls of her upswept hairdo, and . . . one of those *little white dogs* on the end of a leash." More typical, of course, and thus more influential, are such ruminations as these, from "A Wave":

> But for the tender blur
> Of the setting to mean something, words must be ejected
> bodily,
> A certain crispness be avoided . . .

or

                    Much later on
        You thought you perceived a purpose in the game at the
                                                    moment
        Another player broke one of the rules . . . .

Given John Ashbery's acknowledged admiration for Mari-
anne Moore, can this be anything but homage to "An Octo-
pus"? The possibility increases as one considers the following
passage—a crucial one in that it comes close to having a sub-
ject and to saying something about it:

> The cimmerian moment in which all lives, all destinies
> And incompleted destinies were swamped
> As though by a giant wave that picks itself up
> Out of a calm sea and retreats again into nowhere
> Once its damage is done.

It's not simply a matter of a giant wave being like an
avalanche. It's also that nearly toneless timbre, that constitu-
tional reluctance to raise one's voice even at the onset of an
apocalyptic giant wave. This distinctive murmur would seem,
as Bonnie Costello has suggested, to draw upon the example
of Marianne Moore, and from a like fear and dread of all
that Poetry with a capital P has come to stand for. If this
hunch is correct, it would appear that her influence on the
poetry now being written is greater than has been generally
supposed. And if the current rash of affectations is treatable
at all, it can only be so through a renewed attention to its
sources—by paying heed, finally, not to the manner but the
matter of the thing:

> Hands that can grasp, eyes that can dilate, hair that can rise if
> it must, these things are important not because a high sound-
> ing interpretation can be put upon them but because they are
> useful; when they become so derivative as to become unintelli-
> gible, the same thing may be said for all of us—that we do not
> admire what we cannot understand.

I don't think Marianne Moore would have minded having all those line breaks knocked down and plowed into a block of prose for the sake of argument. To be more imitated than read is a worse fate still than to be told that what one writes is not poetry.

The Theatrical Emily Dickinson

The confirmed recluse, the one who

> . . . could not bear to live — aloud
> The racket shamed me so —

is all but fixed in the national hagiography. But Emily Dickinson as a living person, and likewise the sum of what she wrote, were troublesomely various, even to a degree noisy. All this is a matter of record. Decades before Richard Sewall's ordering of that record in *The Life of Emily Dickinson* (Farrar, Straus & Giroux, 1974), and indeed before Thomas H. Johnson gave order to the poems in their presumed entirety (Little, Brown, 1955), in reviewing the letters as edited by Mabel Loomis Todd, Marianne Moore astutely wrote: "A certain buoyancy that creates an effect of inconsequent bravado—a sense of drama with which we may not be quite at home—was for her a part of the breath necessary to existence."

A sense of drama with which we may not be quite at home: an explosiveness, in other words, an excess of feeling as yet unbestowed. One meets with that excess in Emily Dickinson's effort at whimsy when she wrote to her young uncle Joel Norcross, who had evidently promised to write to her in particular but whose letter, when it arrived, was addressed instead to her father:

Adapted from a paper originally presented in October, 1988, and published in the PEN American Center *Newsletter*, May, 1989.

. . . you have sent my father a letter — so there remains no more but to fight. War Sir — "my voice is for war!" Would you like to try a duel — . . . The last duel I fought did'nt [*sic*] take but five minutes in all — the "wrapping the drapery of his couch about him — and lying down to pleasant dreams" included . . . Harm is one of those things that I always mean to keep clear of — but somehow my intentions and me don't chime as they ought. . . .

That was in 1850, when Emily Dickinson was nineteen. The posturing did not diminish with the years; and even as a girl, I think she tended to scare people. She laughed in the wrong places. She raised questions that were not merely impudent but blasphemous:

> Papa above!
> Regard a Mouse
> O'erpowered by the Cat!

That is from poem #61, in Thomas Johnson's numbering. When I asked Richard Sewall about it, he said without hesitation that it couldn't but be a parody of "Our Father who art in Heaven. . . ."

As a girl in her teens, Emily Dickinson had seen dozens of her contemporaries carried away by the evangelical revival that was then in progress. To her, however ardent her nature, the experience of conversion did not come, and it may be that this inner obduracy—something that at least a part of her truly regretted—was what set her on the road to the extreme of wariness recorded by Thomas Wentworth Higginson after he called at the Dickinson homestead one day in August, 1870. She was by then thirty-nine, and

much too enigmatical a being for me to solve in an hour's interview, and an instinct told me that the slightest attempt at direct cross-examination would make her withdraw into her shell; I could not sit still and watch as one does in the woods; I must name my bird without a gun, as recommended by Emerson.

When Emily Dickinson wrote that

> I never spoke — unless addressed
> And then 'twas brief and low —

one can only speculate that she was trying on an attitude, in a desperate effort to discover a place for herself, to envision a fate:

> And if it had not been so far —
> And any one I knew
> Were going — I had often thought
> How noteless — I could die —

But the stance is, or was, only empirical. Years later, according to Thomas Johnson's chronology, she would envision the very opposite of fading away without notice—a release of those erotic forces which, in her own instance, evangelism had failed to harness:

> And do I smile, such cordial light
> Upon the Valley glow —
> It is as a Vesuvian face
> Had let its pleasure through. . . .

These lines are from #754, a poem whose opening, the notorious "My Life had stood — a Loaded Gun —," has triggered such a great deal of (to my mind) inconclusive critical comment. Feminist theorizing, perhaps inevitably, can't leave that gun alone. But David Porter is the only scholar, so far as I know, to connect it with a further passage from the letter to Joel Norcross, about how "one man pointed a loaded gun at a man—and it shot him so that he died—and the people threw the owner of the gun into prison—and afterward hung him for *murder*. Only another victim of the misunderstanding of society."

What all this playing with violence adds up to, it seems to me, is a barely disguised plea to be understood, even a cry for help: Don't you see that what I do and say are beyond my control?

To Samuel Bowles, who may or may not have been the "Master" to whom Emily Dickinson addressed her most anguished pleas for recognition, but who is at any rate a likely candidate, she wrote in early August, 1860: "I am much ashamed. I misbehaved tonight. I would like to sit in the dust. I fear I am your little friend no more, but Mrs. Jim Crow. . . . My friends are very few. I can count them on my fingers — and besides, have fingers to spare."

In one of her breathless addresses to the Master himself, she wrote: "Vesuvius dont talk — Etna dont — one of them — said a syllable — a thousand years ago, and Pompeii heard it, and hid forever — She couldn't look the world in the face, afterward — I suppose — Bashfull Pompeii?"

Hyperbole such as this was a necessity of existence. Nor was Emily Dickinson alone in her quandary. Those volcanic images, that Vesuvian face, recall Margaret Fuller writing in her journal, "I feel all Italy glowing beneath the Saxon crust. . . . I shall burn to ashes if all this smoulders here much longer." The problem of feeling in excess of any available object is one of which women in the nineteenth century were acutely conscious. I think of George Eliot, of Charlotte Brontë, Dorothy Wordsworth, and Alice James. The trouble occasioned by that excess is almost the polar opposite to the experience of Alice James's brother Henry, say, or of T. S. Eliot—neither of whom can be imagined writing, as Emily Dickinson did, "You cannot fold a flood / And put it in a drawer."

Emily Dickinson is all extremes. She could be arch, to a degree that makes a reader uneasy. Smarmy sentiment came to her a bit too easily, and may alas have contributed to her eventual popularity:

> "Hope" is the thing with feathers —
> That perches in the soul —

The anxious cuteness that infects many of her letters ("Was I the little friend — a long time? Was I — Mary?") arises from discomfort, and so do the swagger, the mock threats, and the literary showing-off in the letter to Joel Norcross. "I never felt at Home — Below," she would declare, and there is a kind of cuteness, once again, in what follows:

And in the Handsome Skies
I shall not feel at Home — I know —
I don't like Paradise —

Because it's Sunday — all the time —
And Recess — never comes —

There is impudence in

If God could make a visit —
Or ever took a Nap —
So not to see us —

Then comes a shift, a change of key, and we are in the pres-
ence of what makes Emily Dickinson, for all her skittish insecu-
rity, uniquely a great poet:

but they say
Himself — a Telescope

Perennial beholds us —
Myself would run away
From Him — and Holy Ghost — and All —
But there's the "Judgment Day"!

The moral world as a great, splendid, terrible auditor-
ium—this was the vision by which, it would appear, she staved
off a greater terror, that of vanishing without further notice.
Within that auditorium she saw enacted the drama of the Civil
War. Those who have supposed Emily Dickinson took no inter-
est in day-to-day events could not have been more mistaken.
Shira Wolosky, in *Emily Dickinson: A Voice of War* (Yale, 1971),
points out that of the 1,775 poems now in print, 852, or over
half, have been dated to the years from 1861 to 1865. A
relatively small number of these, it is true, refer specifically
and directly to the conflict itself. But what struck me, in re-
reading them, was how poem after poem is suffused with
awareness of carnage—with references to cannon and bayo-
nets, to the bandaging of wounds: "And tints the transit in the
West / With harrowing iodine" is characteristic in more ways

than one. The hues of sunset, indeed, become all but inseparable from images of bloodshed:

> Whole Gulfs of Red, and Fleets — of Red —
> And Crews — of solid Blood —
> Did place about the West — Tonight —
> As 'twere specific Ground —
>
> And They — appointed Creatures —
> In Authorized Arrays —
> Due—promptly— as a Drama —
> That bows — and disappears—
>
> (#658)

It is as though in such images she had found a subject equal to that sense of drama which Marianne Moore saw as necessary to her existence:

> Like Mighty Foot Lights — burned the Red
> At Bases of the Trees —
> The far Theatricals of Day
> Exhibiting — to These —
>
> 'Twas Universe — that did Applaud —
> While Chiefest — of the Crowd —
> Enabled by his Royal Dress —
> Myself distinguished God —
>
> (#595)

Fame as no plant that grows on mortal soil, as a condition finally indistinguishable from her own solitude—this is the vision by means of which Emily Dickinson's unease in the face of society, the lack of anyone to converse with on her own terms, were ultimately transcended. A sense of audience, with intimations of dispersal, becomes the frame of her own high drama of consciousness:

> Departed — to the Judgment —
> A Mighty Afternoon —
> Great Clouds — like Ushers — leaning —
> Creation — looking on —
>
> (#524)

Space and splendor, here, become her native habitat. At such moments she is unequaled except perhaps by Wordsworth, and surpassed only (just possibly) by the "cloud-capped towers, the gorgeous palaces" evoked by the very master of all things theatrical.

A Poet's Henry James

There is a story Henry James told about himself that sometimes gives me comfort. In his later years he lived mainly at Lamb House, a Georgian landmark in the old town of Rye, on the south coast of England. One day on his usual walk he met a woman he knew he knew, only he couldn't for the life of him think who she was; and he was still wondering how to deal with the situation when she said, "I've done up the joint into rissoles"—and then he knew. She was his housekeeper.

When I made a pilgrimage to Rye a couple of summers ago, it was with the objective of standing on the spot where Henry James dictated *The Ambassadors*. Of course that is not the only novel composed in the garden room at Lamb House; but it was the one I happened at the time to have reread last, and which I had in mind as I stood on that sacred spot. It seemed the more sacred, perhaps, because the garden room itself no longer exists; it was destroyed by a bomb during the Second World War.

The word *sacred* is one James himself used so often that he might be said to have used it to excess. There is a kind of society hyperbole in his diction, and it became more and more pronounced in the works he dictated. But there is a little more than that to his use of the word *sacred,* and it has to do with the reason, or one of the reasons, James moved away from London to the quasi-rural backwater that was Rye. It has to do with what he would later refer to as "the strange sacred time" after he made up his mind to be a playwright. That project

Originally published in the *Southwest Review* (Winter 1991).

turned into a great and terrible disaster, one that had been long in the making. It occurred at the St. James Theatre in London on the evening of January 5, 1895, when his play *Guy Domville* had its opening. What happened, in James's own words, was "an abominable quarter of an hour during which all the forces of civilisation in the house waged a battle with the most gallant, prolonged and sustained applause with the hoots and jeers and catcalls of the roughs, whose roars (like those of a cage of beasts at some infernal 'zoo') were only exacerbated (as it were) by the conflict." That was, as I say, on January 5, 1895; and James had made up his mind to try writing for the stage at least fifteen years earlier, when he wrote in his journal: "The drama is the ripest of the arts" and went on to say, "I think I may now claim to have studied the art as well as it can be studied in the contemplative way. The French stage I have mastered; I say that without hesitation. . . . I knew my chance would come. Here it is; let me guard it *sacredly*."

So there it is again—that word *sacred*. Well, it *is* partly hyperbole. We don't think of Henry James as having precisely ecclesiastical concerns. But wait a minute—long enough to consider what *Guy Domville* was about. Not everybody has bothered to read it, and the truth is that it's not, after all, a very good play. Toward the end of the last act there comes a line—"I am, sir, the last of the Domvilles"—to which, we are told, a voice in the gallery retorted, "And it's a bloody good thing y'are." Who was this poor hero, and what had he done to bring on such hostility? Why, he was a nice young man who believed he had a vocation for the monastic life. And what he did was to waffle repeatedly about whether he would or would not renounce that vocation in order to marry and perpetuate a family line that would otherwise die with him. Well, one can't help thinking that Guy Domville's imaginary dilemma reflected, quite unconsciously, Henry James's own mixed feelings about writing for the stage. Even when he was writing of the dramatic form as "the most beautiful thing possible," he had been constrained to add, "The misery of the thing is that the baseness of the English-speaking stage affords no setting for it."

Be that as it may, I've found it interesting to take note of how often ecclesiastical settings—convents and churches—figure in the work of Henry James. The quintessential "Great Good Place," in the story by that title—of which more later—is only one of many. In *The Tragic Muse*, whose central character is an actress (and which was written during that "strange sacred time" before *Guy Domville* opened), we find a ruined abbey where a more typically Jamesian character gathers courage to give up his seat in Parliament and become a painter. There is the role given to a cloistered setting in *The Portrait of a Lady:*

> "Pansy will never know any harm," said the child's father. "Pansy is a little convent-flower."
> "Oh, the convents, the convents!" cried the Countess, with a sharp laugh. "Speak to me of the convents. You may learn anything there; I am a convent-flower myself. I don't pretend to be good, but the nuns do. . . ."

Toward the end of the novel, when Pansy has been sent off to live with those same nuns, Gilbert Osmond, who has done the sending, observes: "The Catholics are very wise, after all. The convent is a great institution; we can't do without it; . . . It's a school of good manners; it's a school of repose." That is Gilbert Osmond's view, and not necessarily the author's. The view of Isabel Archer (not necessarily his either) is quite different: the convent produces for her "the impression of a well-appointed prison." But the way she views ecclesiastical Rome is less simple. She feels for it nothing like the distaste implicit in *Middlemarch*, for instance, when George Eliot writes that the red draperies at St. Peter's during the Christmas season were "like a disease of the retina." On the contrary,

> the first time [Isabel] found herself beneath the far-arching dome and saw the light drizzle down through the air thickened with incense and with the reflections of marble and gilt, of mosaic and bronze, her conception of greatness received an extension. After this it never lacked space to soar.

There is to come a day, of course, when Isabel finds herself far too much weighed down to soar at all. That tends to be the fate of Henry James's heroines. Take Madame de Vionnet, in *The Ambassadors.* Where do we first begin to see *her* as weighed down but in the cathedral of Notre Dame? A figure "whose supreme stillness" as she sits, evidently "renewing her courage . . . in the sacred shade," attracts the notice of the protagonist Lambert Strether, turns out to be the lady herself. Nor is it only James's female characters who take refuge in "the sacred shade." At a climactic moment in *The Wings of the Dove,* Merton Densher slips into an oratory in the Brompton Road as the most likely place for sorting things out. It happens to be Christmas, there is a service going on, which "didn't match his own day, but . . . was much less of a discord than some other things actual and possible."

These instances are typical of a tendency to be found throughout the novels of Henry James, one which becomes more pronounced in those written after the failure of *Guy Domville.* It is that climactic scenes almost invariably, and most memorably, center on a figure in solitude. Even before *Guy Domville,* we find this figure very memorably indeed in *The Portrait of a Lady:*

> . . . she lingered in the soundless drawing-room long after the fire had gone out. There was no danger of her feeling the cold: she was in a fever. She heard the small hours strike, and then the great ones, but her vigil took no heed of time. Her mind, assailed by visions, was in a state of extraordinary activity. . . . When the clock struck four she got up; she was going to bed at last, for the lamp had long since gone out and the candles had burned down to their sockets. But even then she stopped again in the middle of the room, and stood there gazing at a remembered vision. . . .

It is the remembered vision that counts—the moment of insight into what has gone before. It leaves Isabel Archer, just here, in a state of extreme agitation. But there are great stillnesses for her as well. One that shows James's natural dramatic sense occurs earlier in the novel, when we learn, along with Isabel, of the death of the uncle who will turn out to have left her the fortune from which her later woes depend:

She had placed herself in a deep window-bench, from which she looked out into the dull, damp park; and as the library stood at right angles to the entrance-front of the house, she could see the doctor's dog-cart, which had been waiting for him the last two hours before the door. She was struck with the doctor's waiting so long; but at last she saw him appear in the portico, stand a moment, slowly drawing on his gloves and looking at the knees of his horse, and then get into the vehicle and drive away. Isabel kept her place for half an hour; there was a great stillness in the house. It was so great that when she at last heard a soft, slow step on the deep carpet of the room, she was almost startled by the sound.

This is just as cinematic, in its own way, as the novels of Dickens very often are. What makes it striking, in a writer so garrulous as James, is the absence of dialogue. Here is another such scene, from *The Ambassadors:* Lambert Strether receiving the news that *as* ambassador he has, so to speak, been sacked for incompetence:

He read his telegram in the court, standing still a long time where he had opened it and giving five minutes, afterwards, to the renewed study of it. At last, quickly, he crumpled it up as if to get it out of the way; in spite of which, however, he kept it there—still kept it when, at the end of another turn, he had dropped into a chair placed near a small table. Here, with his scrap of paper compressed in his fist and further concealed by his folding his arms tight, he sat for some time in thought, gazed before him so straight that Waymarsh appeared and approached him without catching his eye. The latter, in fact, struck with his appearance, looked at him hard for a single instant and then, as if determined to that course by some special vividness in it, dropped back into the *salon de lecture* without addressing him.

We never do learn the wording of that telegram. We don't need to. There are times when the spoken word fails, becomes superfluous, amounts to a distraction—if not, for purposes more or less abysmal and nefarious, the deliberate putting on of a mask. And there are times when solitude is of the essence. Here is a scene from *The Wings of the Dove,* after Milly Theale

has paid her crucial visit to the doctor and gone for a walk in
Regent's Park:

> . . . now she knew why she had wanted to come by herself. No
> one in the world could have sufficiently entered into her state;
> no tie would have been close enough to enable a companion to
> walk beside her without some disparity. She literally felt, in this
> first flush, that her only company must be the human race at
> large, present all round her. . . .
> . . . the real thing was to be quite away from the pompous
> roads, well within the centre and on the stretches of shabby
> grass. Here were benches and smutty sheep; here were idle
> lads at games of ball, with their cries mild in the thick air; here
> were wanderers, anxious and tired like herself. . . .
> . . . there was a sort of spell in the sense that nobody in the
> world knew where she was. It was the first time in her life that
> this had happened; somebody, everybody appeared to have
> known before, at every instant of it, where she was; so that she
> was now suddenly able to put it to herself that that hadn't been
> a life.

From this passage we learn enough about Milly's solitude that
James is able to close the door on her as she is dying alone in her
Venetian palace. Moreover, he turns this indirection into a
great dramatic tour de force, with no more by way of an ac-
count of her last days than a figure of speech. When James
writes of two survivors that "they just stood at the door. They
had the sense of the presence within—they felt the charged
stillness; after which . . . they turned away together," he doesn't
mean it literally; the two are in London, waiting for news, and
they are not being altogether straight with each other. But the
figure of speech and what went before it have done their work.
What makes *The Wings of the Dove* not quite like any other of
James's novels is the great stillness that is its center. That may be
why the attempt to turn it into an opera just didn't work. The
scenery is operatic, but the situation isn't. It's like sending Em-
ily Dickinson onto the stage at La Scala. It's a poet's condition,
that stillness. And though in some ways *The Wings of the Dove* is
an anomaly, I think it can still be said that James is a poet's
novelist. Pound observed that James had done things in the

novel that had not yet been attempted in verse. It can't be an accident that he and Eliot each wrote his own portrait of a lady. When you find Madame de Vionnet saying, at her last, desperate interview with Lambert Strether, that "we might, you and I, have been friends," you can hardly doubt where Eliot got his

> "I have been wondering frequently of late
> (But our beginnings never know our ends!)
> Why we have not developed into friends."

To make such a connection, though, is not to say that anybody, in either verse or prose, ought to imitate Henry James. "A very poor model to follow," William Gass has said of him. "He will swallow you up. It's like coming after Milton. Just run as fast in the other direction as you can."

By which William Gass surely did not mean to advocate not reading Henry James. I think he meant rather that you go back and reread because, as with the greatest poets, the experience, the reading itself, turns out to be inexhaustible. You discover so much you'd forgotten, or maybe never noticed before. It can be startling, for instance, to rediscover the way James writes about weather. One might suppose that a writer concerned with the nature of the "felt life," the workings of the mind—a writer who didn't recognize his own housekeeper when he met her in the street—wouldn't have paid the elements all that much attention. But the attention is there. Even in *The Awkward Age*, which consists of dialogue and very little else, the opening page offers a delicious vignette of

> . . . the 'four-wheeler' that, in the empty street, under the glazed radiance, waited and trickled and blackly glittered. The butler mentioned it as, on such a wild night, the only thing they could get, and Vanderbank, having replied that it was exactly what would do best, prepared, in the doorway, to put up his umbrella and dash down to it.

The Ambassadors—and I think this may be one reason it has been my favorite more often than any of the others—is suffused with the meteorological sense of Paris, culminating in the excursion into the countryside where one of the chance encounters that are a favorite device of James's occurs, and where Lambert Strether's view of just about everything is changed forever. In *The Wings of the Dove*, the weather becomes literally a character in the drama with the arrival of "the first sea-storm of autumn," when we find ourselves in "a Venice of cold, lashing rain from a low black sky, of wicked wind raging through narrow passages, of general arrest and interruption." There comes a crucial scene when we hear "in the silence, on the Canal, the renewed downpour of rain." Then, too late to be of any use,

> The weather changed, the stubborn storm yielded, and the autumn sunshine, baffled for many days, but now hot and almost vindictive, came into its own again. . . . Venice glowed and plashed and called and chimed again; the air was like a clap of hands, and the scattered pinks, yellows, blues, seagreens, were like a hanging out of vivid stuffs, a laying down of fine carpets.

Above all and among many other things, *The Wings of the Dove* just now seems to me to be a protracted tribute to the poetry of appearances, of how things look. Appearances as a thing to be kept up are there as well. The notion may be seen as small-minded, but we are shown that that is by no means always so—that keeping up appearances is inseparable from the notion of a civilized life. The meaner side of it is a theme James also treated again and again. He does so devastatingly in the opening scene of the novel, where we are presented with Kate Croy's unspeakable father, who manages somehow to look down on everyone and everything, including the place he happens to be living in. "For a minute after she came in it was as if the place were her *own,* and *he* the visitor with susceptibilities" (my italics). And so it is that we find Kate feeling all over again, with a familiar dismay, "How little his appearance ever by any chance told about him." What she has to deal with, in fact, is a kind of cut-rate Gilbert Osmond, whose entire stock in trade and function in life have been to feel superior. Osmond, as he sends off his daughter to the convent, speaks witheringly of "the manners of the present time" and of "the bustling, pushing rabble, that calls itself society." Lionel Croy does the same when he addresses his daughter as one of "all you hard, hollow people"—and goes on to speak, as Osmond wouldn't have thought of doing, of himself, his appearance that is, as "what's called in the business world, I believe, an 'asset.' . . . Your duty," he tells his daughter, "is to use me. Show family feeling by seeing what I'm good for."

The crassness of this gives dramatic resonance to a later passage, when it is observed of Milly Theale that

> it was of her essence to be peculiarly what the occasion, whatever it might be, demanded when its demand was highest. There were probably ways enough, on these lines, for such a consciousness; another of them would be, for instance, to say that she was made for great social uses. Milly was not wholly sure that she herself knew what great social uses might be . . . .

She learns in due course just what they may be for a girl with a lot of money. But what she does, and what transforms a really low and sordid plot, such as James's novels tend to hang upon, into high drama, is Milly's own determination, at another level from Lionel Croy's, to keep those appearances up. She spends a great deal of money doing it; she turns it into a great performance. She gives a party in her hired Venetian palace, at which she appears wearing pearls, looking wonderful, and being the perfect hostess—all without dropping any hint, though everybody there probably knows it anyhow, that she is what we would now call terminally ill.

Great performances are something we see a lot of in the novels of Henry James, but above all in the later ones. In some ways the greatest of them all is the one turned in by Charlotte Stant, a moneyless, somewhat tarnished but in the end no less put-upon Milly Theale. *The Golden Bowl* is a novel of transcendant deceptions, of lying as a form of magnanimity. One might suppose that a novel about behaving well, no matter what the cost, would be out of date; but this one is not. One of the insights that make reading and rereading Henry James so enthralling is the extent to which we all deal in deceptions—

that we're subject, as James was, to shifts of attitude, so necessary if one is to accommodate oneself to the attitudes of those around one, and to the consequent tergiversations in which one finds oneself enmeshed. Lying and deceit are no less prevalent than they ever were; if they're not in fact more prevalent, an ever proliferating number of channels keep us aware of the things people say in the process of making themselves up, cosmetically and otherwise—of, as T. S. Eliot put it (and almost certainly the debt to James is there too), preparing "a face to meet the faces that you meet." We see a crude but wonderful example of this in *What Maisie Knew*—and when I put it down not long ago, I thought for more than a few minutes that *it* must after all be his masterpiece—when Maisie, after protracted neglect, finds her impossible mother making up to her:

> her huge eyes, her red lips, the intense marks in her face formed an *éclairage* as distinct and public as a lamp set in a window. The child seemed quite to see in it the very beacon that had lighted her path; she suddenly found herself reflecting that it was no wonder the gentlemen were guided. This must have been the way Mamma had first looked at Sir Claude; . . . It must have been the way she looked also at Mr. Perriam, and Lord Eric. . . .

We see another, subtler example of what a performance can be in the climactic scene of *The Ambassadors,* when for a few seconds beside the landing at the little riverside inn, there is a question whether Lambert Strether and the guilty pair, Chad Newsome and Madame de Vionnet, will or will not acknowledge the encounter. Once Strether has settled the matter by hailing them, it is Madame de Vionnet's behavior that sets the tone; and her behavior is a performance from beginning to end.

That life in her stratum of society—even in others less well established, even in the supposedly frank and unfettered realm of childhood behavior—consists of performances, was an insight that had come early to Henry James. It arrived in the person of his little cousin Marie, whom he heard objecting to being sent to bed. On her mother's plea with her not to "make a scene," this is what occurred to the boy Henry James, or so he reported many years after: "Life at these intensities clearly became 'scenes'; but the great thing, the immense illumination, was that we could make them or not as we chose."

No wonder, then, that Edmund Gosse was to describe James in his later years as having the look of an actor. No wonder that James so long felt himself destined to make scenes of his own by the writing of plays. No wonder that we find him recording in his notebook, five years after the failure of *Guy Domville*, his excitement over an invitation from the producer of that same ill-fated piece to try again. He politely declined, but observed:

> It isn't at all the contact with the theatre—still, as ever, strangely odious; it's the contact with the DRAMA, with the divine little difficult, artistic, ingenious, architectural FORM that makes old pulses and old tears rise again.

When it comes to architectural form, no novelist, it seems to me, ever handled it more masterfully. You see this, for example, in the way *The Portrait of a Lady* both opens and closes on the grounds of Gardencourt, where Isabel Archer, as she sits looking out for a long time at the dog-cart by the entrance, absorbs the human drama that is going on within. In the final chapters of the novel we find Isabel once again at Gardencourt, where another death is imminent. The symmetry of this is straightforward enough. But there is also the intensity of the remembered vision. After the death of her cousin, Isabel finds herself near a rustic bench, and it comes to her how she had been sitting there six years before, reading a letter from Caspar Goodwood, her American suitor—and how, looking up, she discovered that she had been followed here by Lord Warburton, who was about to ask her to marry him. "She only stood before it," we are told of this moment six years later, "and while she stood, the past came back in one of those rushing waves of emotion by which people of sensibility are visited at odd hours. The effect of this agitation was a sudden sense of being very tired." She sits down, time passes, and in the dusk she looks up and sees that she is no longer alone. The person who has joined her is Caspar Goodwood. This is the kind of dominant chord that comes naturally to a dramatist, and it came naturally to Henry James. In the later novels, the dramatic resonances are less schematic, more musical; and they are everywhere. I have mentioned the opening scene in *The Wings of the Dove,* between Kate and her awful father. We don't meet with him again directly; but in the novel's penultimate scene we learn that he has appeared at his older daughter's, Kate's sister's door, begging to be taken in. Asked "What does he do?" Kate, who has likewise taken refuge with her sister, answers simply, "He cries."

But that isn't all. Kate's concerted efforts have long been to steer clear of just such surroundings as those in which her lover, Merton Densher, now finds her. "Horrible place, isn't it?" she says. It has occurred to him, indeed, that she has the air of "a distinguished stranger . . . who was making the best of a queer episode and a place of exile." This can't but be heard as a variation, in a still sadder key, of Kate's insight into the way her father once regarded his own living quarters. When the author adds, concerning Densher's reaction to the place, that "at the end of three minutes he felt himself less appointedly a stranger in it than she," the cumulative chord is complete.

Or not really complete after all. It is one of a succession of tones that vibrate through this extraordinarily dense and disturbing episode. Densher finds himself recalling Kate in other settings, among them several in Venice, where they had become lovers. As the interview protracts into silence, another poignant scene recurs:

> He looked out into the lamplit fog, lost himself in the small sordid London street . . . as he had lost himself, in Venice, in the vista of the Grand Canal, that day in the rain.

These modulations, which go to make up the drama of interior awareness, of what goes unsaid, are not of the sort to be rendered in a Puccini aria, or perhaps by the human voice at all. Better suited, perhaps, are the wordless colloquies among the strings in a Mozart quintet. But to do more than say this, to insist on it at all, is to begin to go astray. As Howard Moss in effect declared of the music of Mozart, there is nothing that a Henry James novel is really like. Reading and rereading one of them nevertheless does have something in common with listening to a piece of music. And what I want to add is that for anyone concerned with what used to be called the life of the mind, it is maybe a bit more like what exercises at the barre are for a dancer. More precisely still, periodic rereadings become an antidote to certain prevailing tendencies in what we have to call our culture.

Underlying everything Henry James wrote—underlying the way he dictated in his later years, with all those hesitations, those maddeningly ponderous inversions and circumlocutions—was a conviction that everything is complicated. What we know, and keep being told afresh, about physical structures and interrelations—whether in the environment as a whole or within the walls of a single cell, not to mention the electrochemical reactions that make up our mental processes—would seem to bear him out. All such evidence notwithstanding, there remains a continued unrelenting pressure to regard any insistence that things *are* complicated as either an irrelevance to be brushed aside or, if that can't be done, as somehow an affront, almost as though it were the denial of a birthright. Who has time for complications when everybody knows that time is money?

Well, of course there's nothing new in this complaint. Henry James, with what seems an uncanny prescience, described New York as it was a little after the turn of the century toward whose end we are plunging headlong, with less and less time to spare. The thing that irked him most, apparently, was what (in *The American Scene*) he called "the great religion of the Elevator." In place of the dreamlike leisure of the Old World's grass-grown open-air staircases, he went on to say, the "sempiternal lift" became "an almost intolerable symbol of the herded and driven state and of that malady of preference for gregarious ways, of insistence on gregarious ways only, by which the people about one" even then (to James at least) seemed driven.

When David Riesman published *The Lonely Crowd* back in 1950, it wouldn't have been news to Henry James, however much so it may have been for a lot of other people. And anyhow, the news didn't halt the progress of the malady—one sign or side effect of which is what might be called Disneyitis, the kind of simplification that does away with the *insides* of things: the silly-putty shape with no interior articulation or organs of any kind. Which is not to say that there is no such thing as a noble simplicity. But more than any other, that kind of simplicity entails a degree of solitary brooding, away from what James, once again, identified as "the abject collective consciousness of being pushed and pressed in, . . . with something that slides or slams or bangs, operating, in your ear, as ruthlessly as the guillotine." He was speaking, still, of riding in what, as a typical departure from the Brits, we've chosen to call an elevator; but it could just as well be applied to what the sound bite, and various other slicing mechanisms, have done to the general perception of the passage of time. And he might have had in mind the unending parade of silly-putty figures, along with the smirking human robots that contribute to this same perception, when he referred to the lack of penetralia, of recesses within. When James complained of their absence, he was writing of large public buildings: even the grandest of these, here in America, gave him no sense of inwardness, of space set aside, of stillness at the center.

It was as though the seemingly unlimited spaces of the New World had proved so daunting as not to lend themselves to any true enclosure—or indeed to a sense of the sacred, except as a halfhearted borrowing from the Old World. Having crossed the North American continent during the return visit that produced his complaints about the absence of penetralia, Henry James pronounced it "too *huge* simply, for any human convenience." At Coronado Beach, "in front of this green Pacific," he dreamed of finding himself, "my long dusty adventure over," once again at Lamb House, where his imagination could settle in and get back to work. It had been to escape the distractions of London that he had moved down there, some seven years before. Just how intensely the prospect drew him is hinted at in "The Great Good Place," written during the time immediately before he moved to Rye. In that place—otherwise unnamed except as The Great Want Met—"the inner life woke up again, and it was the inner life, for people of his generation, victims of the modern madness, that was returning health." The protagonist, George Dane, overwhelmed by the demands on him as a successful author, finds himself translated to a "great cloister, enclosed externally on three sides and probably the largest lightest fairest effect . . . that human hands could ever have expressed in dimensions of length and breadth," where "the essence of the bliss" was "precisely that there was nothing now to time."

Such is the nature of all happy visions—one is as though lifted out of time. And so it is with George Dane (whose initials, perhaps not incidentally, are the same as Guy Domville's): when he emerges from his vision, it is with no notion at all of how long he has been beyond the reach of the world—whether for days, weeks, months, or, on the other hand, for no more than two minutes—until he learns, from the visitor who had filled his place meanwhile, that he has been asleep all day. At the day's beginning, it had been raining; and at the end "the rain—the great rain of the night—had come back." He is in the world again, refreshed and ready to resume his place.

Like most of us, Henry James wanted to have things both ways. He was very much a social animal, and being a writer, he could not but crave an audience. But it was in stillness that his own, and his characters', insights came alive. And it is this inwardness, the consciousness of a centered being, that gives his novels their power. It is also what impeded him as a playwright, dramatist though, heartbreakingly, he very nearly was.

"Dearest Edith"

Edith Wharton in later years would write of Henry James as "perhaps the most intimate friend I ever had, though in many ways we were so different." As novelists and as social animals they had, on the contrary, much in common. Wharton herself observed that James "belonged irrevocably to the old America out of which I also came, and of which—almost—it might paradoxically be said that to follow up its last traces one had to come to Europe." Both had nostalgic memories of living abroad as children, and their feelings about the country they had both left but kept returning to, in fact or imagination, were inevitably mixed.

In fact, their return visits twice coincided, and some of the meatiest entries in the *Letters: 1900–1915* of Henry James and Edith Wharton, edited by Lyall H. Powers (Scribner, 1990), were written on American soil. This correspondence, or what remains of it, is so lopsided as hardly to merit the name: as against 167 items signed by James, the volume includes just 29 signed by Wharton—of which meager hoard a mere 13 are addressed to James himself.

Twice—in November, 1909, and again six years later—a despondent James had burned quantities of his papers, among them a good many letters from the younger novelist. Among the earliest of these would have been a note offering good wishes for the opening of his play *Guy Domville*. Wharton's own career as a writer had then no more than been launched; his, as a consequence of that January evening, was to enter what too

Originally published as "At Home and Abroad" in the *New Republic*, June 4, 1990. Reprinted by permission.

few of his readers thought of as its major phase. Lyall Powers dates the meeting that began their friendship to 1903. James was by then sixty-three; Edith Wharton was forty-one. She would later recall that she had already been twice in his presence years before, while she was still in her twenties, and too shy to do more than look her prettiest in the hope of attracting his attention "so that I might at last pluck up courage to blurt out my admiration for *Daisy Miller* and *The Portrait of a Lady.*" Concerning his later work, she would express herself variously. Clearly she had her reservations. But she sent their author her books, he reciprocated with his own—and he was generous as well with literary advice. She *must,* he once declared, "be tethered in native pastures, even if it reduce her to a back-yard in New York."

When James returned to America in August, 1904, for a yearlong stay, he found his protégé in residence, if not exactly tethered, at what was then still her home in the Berkshires. Among the visitors that autumn were Walter Berry, a longtime friend, and Morton Fullerton, a journalist whom she had met through James and who was about to alter her life drastically and forever. The letters James wrote her during this period are still to "Dear Mrs. Wharton," but by the time he found himself a guest of George Vanderbilt, at Biltmore in North Carolina, their tone had grown confidingly expansive. "The mere pen," he declared, ". . . can do but scant justice to the various elements of my situation, the recent, the constant, & the above all acutely—*so* acutely—actual, & that really to talk about them we must take some future N.Y. good fireside hour & then thresh them out to the last straw." It is an instructive pleasure to note the metaphorical vigilance of that "last straw." Whatever his material, James is not going to give himself an easy time. Virtually alone in Vanderbilt's "strange, colossal heart-breaking house, & the desolation & discomfort of the whole thing—whole scene," we see him, after pronouncing it "indescribable," struggling to describe it anyhow: "It's, *in effect,* like a gorgeous practical joke—but at one's own expense, after all, if one has to live in solitude in these leagues-long marble halls, & sit in alternate gothic & Palladian cathedrals, as it were—where now only the temperature stalks about—" and, writer that he is, qualifying as he goes: "In the early spring, I can conceive it as admirable. And I feel that in speaking of it as I have, I don't do justice to the house as a phenomenon (of brute *achievement*)." Compunction sets in: having "been down to luncheon, & been able to see more of the house," he confesses to feeling "a bit shabby at failing to rise to my host's conception."

Ten letters, all neatly turned, several of them substantial, went from James to Wharton during that year of his in America. Back in England, he gave an appearance of having pulled back a little: "You cannot say that I have bombarded you with letters," he begins. Had she perhaps bombarded him? Still ruminating, he takes up the "question of the *roman de moeurs* in America—its deadly difficulty"—to which he has been brought by the concluding installment of *The House of Mirth*. His admiration, though generous, is qualified. "I wish we could talk of it in a motor-car. I have been in motor-cars again, a little, since our wonderful return from Ashfield; but with no such talk as that."

However he might deplore every other form of bustle (for example, the elevator), James at the dawn of our hapless love affair with the internal combustion engine assigned it a rapturously prolonged erotic hyperbole. "The Vehicle of Passion," he called it—or simply "She, the great She."

Passion, of a less whimsical sort, had its part in the intimacy that had begun during a series of daylong expeditions into the Berkshires during the autumn of 1904, and would continue in the French, as well as the English, countryside. Only lately disinterred from the ponderous circumspections of all concerned, Edith Wharton's love affair with Morton Fullerton can be followed here thanks only to the annotations of Professor Powers. Wharton's own memoirs are still more opaque; one could read *A Backward Glance* without guessing that her calamitously troublesome marriage to Teddy Wharton was even unhappy. In James's letters, on the other hand, we see his imagination repeatedly rising to the drama, and to his own role as a kind of Racinian confidant: "Live it all through, every inch of it—out of it something valuable will come—but live it ever so quietly . . . & you'll come down & see me here &

we'll talk à perte de vue, & there will be something in that for both of us."

That was in 1908. Two years later, the roles of confidant and protagonist had undergone what amounted to a convergence. The New York Edition of James's works, on which he had concentrated large hopes and energies, had been a financial disaster; added to his own increasingly frequent bouts of illness and depression had been alarm over the decline of his older brother—and arch rival—William, who was to die at Chocorua, New Hampshire, on August 26, 1910. A series of letters to the confidant who was now "Dearest Edith" records his sitting there "stricken & in darkness"; "the difference in the world & the whole aspect of life [made] by the extinction of his so cherished & dominant presence"; and how "My beloved brother's death has cut into me, deep down, even as an absolute mutilation." Still in New Hampshire with his brother's family, he observes:

> You may say that *any* stay, no matter how long, in our unspeakable country is a scant value—though, just now, in this gorgeous & so native weather with the great chamber of nature hung about as with some embossed & gilded crimsoned and purpled cuir de Cordoue. . . . However, the great matter is that if you really *are* to sail on the deplorable Oct. 15th we absolutely must meet before.

The proposed meeting did take place as Edith Wharton dined in New York with Henry James and, once again, Walter Berry and Morton Fullerton. Teddy Wharton, with whom she had patched things up again one more time, had just departed on a world tour. The strain upon her emotional resources is unrecorded; but it must have been great as she herself prepared to sail for Europe after that gathering in New York. Henry James had more than once, in his half-teasing admiration, called Edith Wharton "terrible"—had called her (even) "the Angel of Devastation." In fact, the devastations of her own life during this period were such as to have undone forever a woman of less fortitude. She had learned of embezzlements and other escapades on the part of her husband, and of her lover Morton Fullerton's equally if not more unsavory past; the love affair itself was already coming to an end, while she shifted households and twice crossed the Atlantic, in addition to the usual motorized hurtlings across the map of England and the Continent. It is no wonder that on her return to Paris she broke down completely. When her writings at the time are taken into account, her endurance up until that moment appears not so much prodigious as demonic. Besides working sporadically at *The Custom of the Country*, in that year she had also published a collection of ghost stories and another of poetry. By December, 1910, only weeks after her collapse, she would be at work again on a story, which grew to the length of a novella and began appearing the following summer. Its title was *Ethan Frome*.

In reading James's letters it is hard not to link this famous tale to a passage dating to November, 1906:

> I am wondering if you are not feeling just now perhaps a good deal, at Lenox, in the apparently delightful old 1840 way—a good snowstorm aiding. . . . But how I want to have it all—the gossip of the countryside—from you! Some of it has come to me as rather dreadful . . . —& that is what some of the lone houses in the deep valleys we motored through used to make me think of!

Wharton, in *A Backward Glance*, would recall that the first pages of *Ethan Frome* had originally been written, in French, purely as an exercise, some years before. The motor-car had made the project possible:

> In those epic days roads and motors were an equally unknown quantity, and one set out on a ten-mile run with more apprehension than would now attend a journey across Africa. But the range of country-lovers like myself had hitherto been so limited, and our imagination so tantalized by the mystery beyond the next blue hills, that there was inexhaustible delight in penetrating to the remoter parts of Massachusetts and New Hampshire, discovering derelict villages with Georgian churches and balustraded house-fronts, exploring slumbrous mountain valleys, and coming back weary but laden with a new harvest of beauty,

after sticking fast in ruts, having to push the car up hill, to rout out the village blacksmith for repairs, and suffer the jeers of horse-drawn travellers trotting gaily past us.

The pleasures of the house at Lenox were such that had it not been for her husband's inability to settle anywhere, Edith Wharton might very well have established herself there. It was otherwise for Henry James. He could write eloquently of the New England countryside; but he referred to "repatriation" as "a mere lurid dream," and it is the testimony of Wharton in *A Backward Glance* that "he was never really happy or at home" in America.

Given the virtual absence of her letters from Professor Powers's collection, the inclusion of *A Backward Glance* in the latest volume of the Library of America amounts to a happy accident. To a total of eight novellas the editor, Cynthia Griffin Wolff, has appended a hitherto unpublished, and rather more forthcoming, autobiographical fragment, entitled *Life and I.* It unfortunately breaks off early. Though in *A Backward Glance* Wharton writes at entertaining length of her friendship with James, one could wish for a bit more of the candor with which she recorded, in that late fragment, her dislike of the company of other little girls, as well as her early propensities as a storyteller:

> Never shall I forget the long-drawn weariness of the hours passed with "nice" little girls . . . when the "pull" became too strong, I would politely ask my unsuspecting companions to excuse me while I "went to speak to mamma," & dashing into the drawing-room I would pant out, "Mamma, please go & amuse those children. *I must make up.*" . . . Oh, the exquisite relief of those moments of escape from the effort of trying to "be like other children"!

More poignant still is the recollection of how "a penetrating sense of 'not-niceness' " kept her from pursuing any inquiry about where babies came from until the very eve of her own marriage, when "I was seized with such a dread of the whole dark mystery, that I summoned up courage to appeal to my mother, & begged her . . . to tell me 'what being married was like.' " This time, disapproval could not stifle the fearful need to know what was about to happen to herself:

> The coldness of her expression deepened to disgust. She was silent for a dreadful moment; then she said with an effort: "You've seen enough pictures & statues in your life. Haven't you noticed that men are—made differently from women?"

Edith Wharton was by then twenty-three. She had resolved, many years later, to set down this harrowing conversation "because the training of which it was the dreadful and logical conclusion did more than anything else to falsify and misdirect my whole life." Bravely though she goes on to insist that "in the end" her life was neither falsified nor misdirected, the cost is unmistakable. That cost, it may be added, also gives strength to her most memorable work. Those of her female characters whom experience does not finally destroy, as it destroys Lily Bart in *The House of Mirth*, emerge maimed and wary, if not literally paralyzed or otherwise locked into the stasis of futility. Such is the fate of Mattie Silver in *Ethan Frome*, of Charity Royall in *Summer*, of Sophy Viner in *The Reef*, of Kate Clephane in *The Mother's Recompense*—all victims to some degree of their own generous impulses. A different kind of character, who seems especially, and touchingly, close to Wharton's own experience, is that of Anna, in *The Reef*. She learns how her lover entered into a casual affair while he was waiting for her answer to his proposal of marriage and, out of the virginal bewilderment of generations of women who have married and borne children without any recompense of physical enjoyment, pleads to be told, "Do such things happen to men often?"

Henry James in a letter dated December, 1912, declared *The Reef* "quite the finest thing you have done; both *more* done than even the best of your other doing, and more worth it through intrinsic value, interest and beauty." He read it, he said, "as a Drama, and almost, as it seems to me, one of psychologic Racinian unity, intensity and gracility." Even here, the praise is qualified: "I'm not sure [Anna's] oscillations are not beyond our notation" is a politer way of registering what a reader cannot but feel, that Anna's decisions and revisions, moment by moment and reversal by reversal, go on more than a few pages too long—as one does *not* feel in the process by which a Jamesian consciousness unfolds.

Still later, at any rate, James would bestow an equal praise on the very different, and in its way more accomplished *Custom of the Country:* "I hang on the sequences," he wrote, "with a beating heart & *such* a sense of your craft, your cunning, your devilish resources in the perpetration of them." By now his protégé has indeed become his "Dear and admirable Confrère."

He had likewise admired *Ethan Frome,* for its "art & tone & truth—a beautiful artful *kept-downness,* & yet effective cumulation." I find myself regretting that he did not live to respond to the companion and counterpart of that bleak winter's tale, the less often reprinted *Summer.* Like *Ethan Frome,* it was written in France. By then Europe was at war, and Edith Wharton's demonic energies had been channeled into a tornado of volunteer work for the Red Cross—first in setting up a workroom for women whose livelihood had been cut off by the fighting, then in fund-raising for Belgian refugees, then in seeing to the needs of military hospitals, among still other projects. "After two years," she wrote, "we all became strangely inured to a state which at first made intellectual detachment impossible. . . . All the pessimism and lamentation," she added, "came from the idlers, while those who were laboring to the limits possessed their souls."

It was in this mental state that she began to write, "at a high pitch of creative joy, but amid a thousand interruptions, and while the rest of my being was steeped in the tragic realities of the war; yet I do not remember ever visualizing with more intensity the inner scene, or the creatures peopling it."

This estimate seems borne out by the story itself. At once idyllic and shocking, *Summer* as a whole is as though drenched in radiance, the poetry of what cannot last. Through the kind of imaginative projection that permitted George Eliot to endow, improbably, a Hetty Sorel or a Gwendolen Harleth with so much of herself, in *Summer* Edith Wharton seems to have given to the figure of Charity Royall, the backwoods foundling whose dream of rising in the world is over when the season ends, the unstinted richness of her own emotional awakening. It had been the desire of each—as Wharton confessed of herself—"to love and to look pretty." Rare is the woman who can free herself of that desire, and this Edith Wharton was clearheaded enough to acknowledge. The story of Charity Royall's own awakening and abandonment seems almost to tell itself, without any of those stretches of insipid dialogue that weaken the fabric of so many Wharton narratives, and with such vividness that we become increasingly agitated participants in the process. What makes *Summer* more than a painful exposé, finally, of what men do to women is the unfolding character of the crude but not simple guardian with whom Charity's fate is entangled. "Lawyer Royall" is indeed the most complex and disturbing of several elderly male characters who add ballast to her later fiction. What would Henry James have made of him? But by the end of February, 1916, he was dead.

His letters to Edith Wharton continued through September, 1915. A number of them were typed from his dictation. His concern was now mainly, sometimes feverishly, with the progress of the war. Her letters to him were now zealously preserved, and handed about. Such first-hand reporting as this, from a letter dated Verdun, February 28, 1915, was bound to have been circulated:

> We went on to Verdun after lunch, stopping at Blercourt to see a touching little ambulance where the sick and nervously shattered are sent till they can be moved. Most of them are in the village church, four rows of beds down the nave, & when we went in the curé was just ringing the bell for vespers. Then he went & put on his vestments, & reappeared at the lighted altar with his acolyte, & incense began to float over the pale heads on the pillows, & the villagers came into the church, &, standing between the beds, sang a strange wailing thing that repeats at the end of every verse:
> "Sauvez, sauvez la France,
> Ne l'abandonnez pas"—It was poignant.

To this, in a hand-written letter, James responded:

. . . your impression is rendered in a degree so vivid & touching that it all (especially those vespers in the church with the tragic beds in the aisles) wrings tears from my aged eyes. What a hungry *luxury* to be able to come back with things & give them then & there straight into the aching voids: do it, *do* it, my blest Edith, for all you're worth: rather, rather—"sauvez, sauvez la France!" Ah, je la sauverais bien, moi, if I hadn't been ruined myself too soon!

That was in March. In October Wharton crossed the Channel and saw him for the last time. It had seemed, she would write many years afterward, "as though a man of his powerful frame and unimpaired intellectual vitality ought to have lived longer." But he had—as she observed—been shaken by the death of his brother, as well as weakened by the disappointment of his long-held hope of becoming a successful dramatist. In the end, though, as she wrote in *A Backward Glance*, "what really gave him his death-blow was the war. He struggled through two years of it, then veiled his eyes from the endless perspective of destruction. It was the gesture of Agamemnon, covering his face with his cloak before the unbearable."

In December, 1915, when word came that Henry James was unmistakably dying, Edith Wharton wrote, "His friendship was the pride and honour of my life." There is in this more than the hyperbole of grief. Their friendship had been as full of nuance and complexity as it was in the end deeply rooted. All of Henry James's own ambivalences toward women, especially women of force and determination, were set quivering by the "Dearest Edith" of whom he could write that she "rode the whirlwind, she played with the storm, she laid waste whatever of the land the other raging elements had spared"—and to whom he would comically admit "the desire, the frantic impulse of scared childhood, to plunge my head under the bed-clothes & burrow there, not to let it (i.e. Her!) get me!"

By "Her" he only partly meant "Dearest Edith's" omnipresently seductive motor-car. This kind of badinage runs at one level all through their correspondence. "The real marriage of two minds," she observed, "is for any two people to possess a sense of humour or irony pitched in exactly the same key."

But what gives life, now, to the surviving correspondence between Edith Wharton and Henry James, thanks to the available supplements and annotations that enable one to enter into the sympathies of both participants, is the largeness of James's own thwarted but still powerful dramatic sense. His long letter of praise for *The Reef,* written in December, 1912, rose finally into a passage Edith Wharton must have treasured for the rest of her life:

> There used to be little notes in you that were like fine benevolent finger-marks, of the good George Eliot—the echo of much reading of that excellent woman here and there, that is, sounding through. But now you are like a lost and recovered "ancient" whom *she* might have got a reading of (especially were he a Greek) and of whom in *her* texture some weaker reflection were to show. For, dearest Edith, you are stronger and firmer and finer than all of them put together. . . . Clearly you have only to pull, and everything will come.

It may be said that nothing in Edith Wharton's large fictional output after her "cher Maître" was gone quite measured up to this noble (though even here, inevitably qualified) hyperbole. She kept at it, writing book after book on lives briefly raised out of, and then reclaimed by, the stasis of convention, in New York or on the French Riviera, or both. It is regrettable, if not really surprising, that *The Mother's Recompense,* the last of the novellas in the Library of America selection, though expertly framed in the stasis she knew all too well, reads like a soap opera. Henry James himself was not always at his best. Edith Wharton is most intensely so in exploring the specific quality of the pain that comes of being a woman. In this she is unsurpassed except by George Eliot at *her* most intense. The intuitive genius of Henry James approached that pain in a manner uniquely his own, and in so doing raised it to a higher level of dramatic art. But of the depth of that intuition there can be no doubt, and it was at such depths, finally, that his friendship with Edith Wharton most freely moved. This is evident from a letter addressed to his "dear and admirable Confrère," a few weeks after the one just quoted: "I can't possibly not want to thank you on the spot for your so deeply interesting and moving letter, this morning received," it begins, and later declares that "you will see and feel what I mean—being about the only person who ever does, in general."

The occasion, we learn from the notes, is that Teddy Wharton's behavior having become egregious, she was finally about to sue for divorce. In concluding, "Je vous embrasse & am all devotedly yr. H J.," the signer had (as so often in his fiction) filled an empty form and left it brimming with his own reality. All her life, she had preferred the company of men. Unlike most of those she had known, he was there when she needed him.

Purloined Sincerity

The writing of letters—real old-fashioned ones, as distinguished from the copiously scripted and distributed appeal to its recipients' worse or better instincts, or even to both at once, that like weeds in an untended plot may soon crowd out all else—is a dying art. To call it an old-fashioned one is not, of course, quite accurate: what survives of early cuneiform and Linear B consists largely, I believe, of commercial inventories, and in any event the once inseparable arts of poetry and music would have existed long before anyone but a few scribes had the means of setting down a line of verse. Moreover, if the numbers who go about with ears engrafted to the headphones of a Walkman are indicative, it seems likely that those same arts, inseparable in their decadence as at the dawn of Western culture, will be with us for as long as the culture itself survives. By comparison, the tenure of the epistolary art will have been brief.

The fifteen essays in *Writing the Female Voice: Essays on Epistolary Literature,* edited by Elizabeth C. Goldsmith (Northeastern University Press, 1989) are concerned in one way or another with letters either actually or purportedly written by women, throughout a period extending from the late sixteenth century into the imagined future. Works published in the eighteenth century are most prominently represented—those not only of Richardson, Cleland, Choderlos de Laclos, and Montesquieu, but also less well-known authors who happened to be women: Sophie LaRoche in Germany and Françoise de Graffigny in

Originally published in the *Kenyon Review* (Fall 1989).

France, among others. The most recent and most forward-looking book to be discussed (in an essay by Linda Kauffman) is Margaret Atwood's *The Handmaid's Tale,* whose epistolary format is that of a cache of tape-recorded messages uncovered and edited by a male archivist in the twenty-first century. The latter's purported commentary gives a final ironic twist to the genre. For its original model, to which many of the essays refer, this form of storytelling goes back to the *Heroides* of Ovid—a collection of letters purportedly written by women ("heroines") actual or mythical (Dido, Sappho, Medea, Circe, Ariadne) to the lovers who have seduced and then abandoned them. Elizabeth Goldsmith in her introduction refers to "the female letter of suffering and victimization" as a "standard *topos* of epistolary literature." The scholarship concerning it has here been laced and corseted by the jargon of the gender study—sexual power structures, the traffic-in-women paradigm, male scopic pleasure, and so on—with a further underpinning of critical terms—construct, thematics, closure, teleology, counterreading, overdetermination, fall into (or is it out of?) language—which tend to make a naive reader restive.*
Whatever value there may be in referring to that paragon of female turpitude, the Marquise de Merteuil, as having an "immense epistemological advantage" over little Cécile Volanges, the naive reader's response is likely to be: Huh? Oh, you mean she *knows* more! And sure enough, we are then told that "Merteuil possesses knowledge of vital interest to Cécile, Cécile knowledge of no interest whatsoever to Merteuil."

---

*An essay by Alicia Borinsky, in the final section of this book, has to do with a quasi-epistolary work, *La Carte Postale,* by Jacques Derrida, whose conceit is not only to be unreadable but also to suppress the female side of the purported correspondence. "The praise for the woman in Derrida's book is, in the last analysis," according to a footnote, "a celebration of her silence, of her capacity to elicit passion through passivity." The author somewhat delphically adds: "Although Derrida has become increasingly aware of the polemical field opened up by the attention to gender, his texts tend to mention it in a mode that is more self-critical than analytical." Whoever may be tempted by his method will at any rate have been warned.

However all this may be, and no matter how arid the vocabulary, the recurring theme of these essays is worth notice. One conclusion, to which all the contributors apparently subscribe, is (as stated by the editor) that "to study the history of the female epistolary voice . . . is to record the ways in which it has been silenced." If this rather sweepingly oversimplifies a situation of real complexity, the record on which it is based is enough to inspire a female reader, at the very least, with a vicarious spasm of rage.

What is to be made, for example, of the *Lettres portugaises,* first offered in 1669 as the authentic outpourings of one Mariane, a Portuguese nun, to the Frenchman who had seduced her, which—as Katharine Jensen's essay informs us—went through twenty-one editions in just five years? Whoever all those readers may have been, their interest could hardly have been otherwise than prurient, if not downright pornographic. That an unfortunate woman's plight, exposed, should become a marketable commodity (without, in those days, the solace of a share in the royalties), is deplorable enough. Compounding the offense is recent evidence that no such person ever existed, except as the fabrication of a male author. A footnote suggests that the issue is still unsettled. Assuming that Mariane is a fiction, it becomes not one woman but all of us who have been had—or, to put it in Katharine Jensen's words, what we have here is an episode in the "larger, more subtle story of men's appropriation and publication of the feminine epistolary text." Although by the seventeenth century numbers of women had written letters and published them under their own names—for example, the sixteenth-century Venetian courtesan, Veronica Franco, whose work is the subject here of an essay by Margaret Rosenthal—there were powerful inhibitions against so doing. As Elizabeth Goldsmith neatly puts it, "A woman's special epistolary talent was seen to reside in her ability to produce convincing and authentic letters of passion, while such a letter was precisely the sort of text that a woman was not supposed to write in the first place." Women might be, and in many quarters were, reputed to excel in the writing of letters; but the manuals, or "secretaries," that offered models of the art, though intended for the use of both sexes, were all edited and largely written by men. Samuel Richardson, whose career as an epistolary novelist began in precisely this way, is one overweening example among many. But no history of manners is ever simple, and it must be added that on the Continent this form of telling women what to do is seen as a reaction to the hold of *galanterie,* an elaborate set of rules legislated in the salons that in the earlier years of the seventeenth century had dominated court life in France—salons which, we are told, were themselves a reaction against the crudeness of the court under Henri IV.

That privileged females are capable of their own tactics and devices, and indeed have had their victories, in the long war between the sexes, is not easily deniable. There remain, on the other hand, those direr aspects of the struggle concerning which women themselves had not had the opportunity to say a great deal in print, and to which the notion of tactics is irrelevant. Concerning those aspects, the eloquence of Alice Walker's *The Color Purple* receives brisk and straightforward notice in the essay by Carolyn Williams that concludes the volume. It may be said in general, I think, that what drives women up the wall, what makes feminists of them when they are compelled to think about it, is the sheer ubiquity of the advantage men have had to start with. Until quite recently— and nobody can say with certainty that its hold has been very much loosened—the hardest to deal with, hence the most oppressive, has been the male tendency to define women's true nature for them. "Artless, gentle, timid, soft, sincere, compassionate; awake to all the finer impressions of tenderness, and melting with pity for every human woe": thus a male character in one epistolary novel, as quoted by Patricia Meyer Spacks.

Compliance with such an ideal, it must be said, is seldom total. Patricia Spacks notes further "the resentment with which women internalized social norms"—this in connection with *Lady Susan,* Jane Austen's one epistolary novel, which depicts a woman in conscious rebellion against those norms. "I am tired of submitting my will to the Caprices of others," Lady Susan declares to her confidant. Excerpted, this might seem to be on the side of the angels. But what the context reveals is a bad mother, a schemer no less than Henry James's Madame Merle, or even (as the author of the essay herself suggests) than Richardson's own prodigiously resourceful Lovelace.

Jane Austen had an intelligence too coolly subversive to be taken in by preconceived notions of anything, including femininity. But few women from her day to this one have been so well equipped as to elude being trapped by other people's expectations. It is in flight from just such a quandary that Clarissa, hemmed in by her own reputation for ladylike behavior, becomes the quintessential victim: the expectation on the part of others that she will comply with arrangements that have been made for her is so much a matter of course that her refusal, with all its protracted reasoning, its alternative proposals, turns her into something like a monster.

The moral claustrophobia to which Clarissa is subjected is an atmosphere familiar enough in twentieth-century writers, and one that is poignantly evoked in the novels of George Eliot; but not even Kafka can have surpassed the elaborateness with which Samuel Richardson spelled out and finally drove into the ground the ways in which women were and still are imposed on.

How can this be? What is it that enabled a mere female impersonator to speak so persuasively on this subject? James Carson, addressing himself to the category identified as Narrative Cross-Dressing in the novels of Richardson, supplies some possible reasons, and it is not without relevance that he is the sole male scholar to be represented here. Employing a phrase from the work of a female one, Nancy Miller, he observes:

One of the constraints on discourse is "the *power* of the female" within, but not completely in the control of, the male imagination. The male anxieties about authorship revealed through authorial self-criticism are not merely evidence for a theory about the dissolution of the subject, a theory that could easily coexist with dominance over and violence against women. Rather the practical power relations between the sexes are determined precisely by the answer to such questions as what an author is, what moral, intellectual, or social qualifications are necessary to fulfill the authorial function.

According to James Carson's argument, self-criticism becomes inseparable from the license of the masquerade, or from the anxiety of the closet transvestite—to which may be added Richardson's own anxiety over his status in relation to the titled ladies with whom he exchanged letters, and his awareness at the same time of his own advantage as a male. Such ambiguity would keep a certain kind of intelligence on the alert to a degree unlikely in those whose circumstances were more clear-cut. Richardson is in the position, on the one hand, of little Miss Churm, Henry James's freckled cockney, who with her love of the theater and her seven sisters (the analogue of Richardson's own houseful of women) could represent virtually anything, as opposed to the Real Thing that couldn't represent even itself; and on the other, of the Spoiled Rich Kid, the white jazzman just out of Princeton.

An exasperation over the notion of entrenched privilege informs the work of contemporary polemicists on behalf of women such as Andrea Dworkin and Catharine MacKinnon. Their discourse, in all its exasperation, seems almost to be taking place in the same airless corridors as those from which Clarissa found no escape. If the truth is, as Catharine MacKinnon has famously asserted, that intimacy (so called) amounts every time to an invasion, the prospect for improved relations would appear to be small. Admittedly, there are times when any one of us may be ready to conclude that what we thought was the nightmare is in fact the reality. As Richardson himself acknowledged in a letter, "Men are naturall Incroachers." And as Adrienne Rich has more lately called on her readers to acknowledge, the amount of lying by women, to one another and to themselves, so as to get from one thing to the next, from one day to another, is almost too much to bear thinking of. One brought up female, even one who regards herself as on the whole fortunate, is likely to writhe at times over a retrospect of false positions, paralyzed waiting, energies squandered, the unending preoccupation with needing to accommodate the fact of gender. From what I have been told, at least some males, if they do not writhe equally, have been similarly uncomfortable. Though some rapprochement may come of turning Gender Studies into an academic discipline, the prospects are far from unclouded.

In a recent story by John Updike, the sum of a lifetime's wisdom, arrived at after an all too recognizable encounter from behind the wheel of a car, is that "pure intimidation and pretension" are "the aim of almost all human behavior." A man's observation concerning other men, younger ones. As though to underscore so bleak an insight, a group of still younger males—most of them too young to possess a driver's license—randomly set upon whatever victim their paths may cross, the climactic one being inevitably a woman, who is beaten, gang-raped, and left for dead.

Further along in the Updike story, which levels off into a mild grouse against women, or rather the kind of woman wives turn into, the protagonist's wife declares, "It's horrible, the way television has turned violence into a joke." The husband offers no argument, the wife having walked out of the room. What more is there to say? We are already repeating ourselves.

It is, as I see it, part of the continuing attrition of civility that fewer and fewer people, even literate ones, write letters any more. Does it matter? Richardson, for one, would say it did. Never mind the shambles of lying and manipulation wrought by the schemers of *Les Liaisons Dangereuses,* or by Lovelace himself. James Carson quotes in his essay Richardson's own assertion that "the pen is jealous of company. It expects, as I may say, to engross the writer's whole self," and goes on to note how in a Richardson novel the writing of letters becomes "a form of self-examination and moral accounting, a delivery over of one's whole self to the confidant for correction." James Carson sees this as "one of several Protestant equivalents for the Roman Catholic confession." The exchanges between Clarissa and her friend Miss Howe are distinguished from such transactions, including those of psychiatry, in being genuinely equal—suggesting, in their minutely interminable obsessiveness, what two reasonably clearheaded and articulate young women might say in a daily session over the telephone. Or would have been saying, but for the engrossings of a syntax that no longer flourishes. Perhaps the withering away of the personal letter is—literally—connected to the withering of that syntax. Or perhaps what is happening is a more drastic and fundamental withering away of communication itself—of the individual and particular transaction, as distinguished from that imposed by the Media, so called—the term having been compacted into the singular by a grammatical solecism even as, in the plural, *they* extend what may perhaps be referred to as their immense epistemological advantage. That direct address is on the wane would be hard to deny since Samuel Beckett—long before *The Handmaid's Tale,* among others, made use of the same device—had the far-seeing wit to extract high drama from a lone man's transactions with a tape recorder.

In any event, an epistolary Gresham's Law would appear to be in effect. What has been happening to the postal service, if not to direct address itself, may be seen, after the manner of bad money driving out good, as one more process of appropriation: junk mail taking over the domain of the personal letter. Viewed in this light, the tendency of members of the teaching-and-essay-writing community to resort to an argot of their own appears no more than a harmless, perhaps even a necessary form of reassurance. And perhaps it is no more than a like, if more desperate, instinct for self-preservation that has turned poetry (so called, and as distinguished from the aural ubiquity made possible by the tape recorder) into little more than an overheard murmur. If people have less and less to say to one another, it may be thanks to the omnipresence of messages that turn out to be junk.

If this is in any degree true, the heavyhandedness, the huckstered unction, the purloined sincerity that now clog every medium, including the one known, with exquisitely unintended irony, as personalized direct mail, may be regarded as a kind of ultimate extension of the process traced by the essays in *Writing the Female Voice*—that is, the longtime propensity of whoever is in a position of advantage to manipulate the forms of direct address in order to enhance that position. As one aspect of the simian urge to grab and fiddle with whatever comes within reach, this is not exactly news. But the oldest human traits are perennially subject to fresh examination. The one we are given here would have been more generally persuasive if the rhetoric employed did not tend to muddy the distinction between real harm and mere pique. (It's not fair. I won't play!) What is happening to letters, of whatever sort, is bad news enough.

The Long, Long Wait: The Epistles
to the Thessalonians

In the Sunday school of my childhood, chanting the names of the books of the Bible was a favored learning device, and up to a point anyhow, it worked. I can still hear "Joshua, Judges, Ruth"; "Isaiah, Jeremiah, Ezekiel"; and likewise "Acts, Romans, First-and-Second-Corinthians." Beyond such clusters of three, I tended to stumble. What I did not learn, and what needs to be digested before one can begin to consider the Epistles of Paul to the Thessalonians, is that chronologically we had the New Testament all wrong. It's not only that of the four Gospels, Mark is earlier than Matthew, and John comes a long, long way after. It's also that Paul's first Epistle to the Thessalonians turns out to have been written before any of the four Gospels: chronologically, it is the earliest book in the entire New Testament.

The ramifications of this discovery are not to be perceived at a glance. They need tracing and pinning down. The date, first of all, is around A.D. 50—that is, approximately twenty years after Jesus of Nazareth was arrested and put to death on a charge of sedition. Paul's earliest Epistle is also the earliest known document to mention Jesus by name. Not only was there no written account of his life and sayings; the word "Christian" had yet to be invented. That the religion it has come to designate would one day be the official cult of the Roman Empire, or an official

Reprinted from *Incarnation: Contemporary Writers on the New Testament*, edited by Alfred Corn, copyright © 1990 by Viking Penguin Inc., a division of Penguin USA Inc.

cult of any kind, would hardly have occurred to anyone. Among dozens of religions, in a period rife with initiations and secret gatherings, a more likely candidate—or so historians tell us—would have been the worship of the Persian god Mithra. At all events, the founding of an official religion was not what the Apostle had in mind when he announced himself, along with two colleagues, in the earliest known Christian document: "Paul, and Silvanus, and Timothy, unto the church of the Thessalonians in God the Father and the Lord Jesus Christ." To know even dimly what he did have in mind, the words he used need to be looked at closely. In A.D. 50 the entire congeries of domes, steeples, gargoyles, stained glass, choir robes, candles—whatever is automatically summoned up by the English word *church*—was far in the future; and equally so was the monolithic hierarchy that springs to mind when the word is written with a capital. The Greek word *ekklesia*, which Paul used, originally had no such associations, any more than the word *synagoge*, which is to be found elsewhere in the New Testament. The word *synagoge* meant originally a gathering, a bringing together; *ekklesia* referred, somewhat more specifically, to a civic assembly. The assembly of believers whom Paul addressed at Thessalonica met in one another's households, as any newly formed, essentially subversive group did then, or would do now.

As Paul uses it, however, the word *ekklesia* is qualified: he writes to the church of the Thessalonians *in*—or, as a more recent translation has it, the church *founded on*—God the Father and the Lord Jesus Christ. The etymological subtleties of this formulation, and more particularly of the phrase *in Christ,* which Paul uses again and again, have been the subject of long and earnest debate, among those for whom the word *christos* itself would call for none. For the rest of us, it needs likewise to be looked at. The literal meaning of *christos* is "anointed one," from a verb meaning "to be rubbed" (most commonly with an oil or salve). It is the Greek equivalent of the Hebrew word *messiah,* similarly derived from a verb meaning "to anoint." Among the Jews up until the time of the Babylonian exile, the word *messiah* referred to one of the kingly line of David, whose anointing by a priest or prophet was taken as a sign that he had been chosen by the Almighty to rule over the children of Israel. By the time of Paul, to pronounce the word *messiah* was to set loose a flood of religious and political overtones: when the Messiah came, it would be as a liberator of the Jews, bringing centuries of foreign domination to an end.

The Thessalonians to whom Paul was writing were not Jews, however. They were ethnic Greeks—sometime pagans who had turned, in the Apostle's words, "from idols, to serve a living and true God." The Greek word *eidolon,* which Paul used, derives from a verb meaning simply "to see," and denotes a thing seen, an image. Among the Jews the worship of such images was of course proscribed. And it had been regarded with particular horror since the Hellenistic Syrian tyrant Antiochus IV had desecrated the Temple at Jerusalem by setting up there an altar to the Olympian Zeus, whose image was enshrined in many a Greek holy place. The view of the world the converts at Thessalonica had accepted, in turning away from all such worship, was essentially a Jewish one. As set forth by the Hebrew prophets, that view had at once a severity and an Oriental excess such as the Greeks, in their concern for balance and clarity, would have put in its place by making it into an art form—ritual drama or a graven image. The Hebrew prophets had no time for art forms. Their message was far too urgent:

> Blow ye the trumpet in Zion, and sound an alarm in my holy mountain; let all the inhabitants of the land tremble; for the day of the Lord cometh, for it is nigh at hand. (Joel 2:1)

Thus the prophet Joel, calling on a backsliding Israel to repent and mend her ways. The Hebrew Bible resounds with such summonings. Here is the prophet Jeremiah on the subject of those heathen art forms:

> Behold the voice of the cry of the daughter of my country because of them that dwell in a far country: Is not the Lord in Zion? Is not her king in her? Why have they provoked me to anger with their graven images, and their strange vanities? (Jeremiah 8:22)

And here is Isaiah taking up the ageless prophetic denunciation:

> Howl ye; for the day of the Lord is at hand; it shall come as a destruction from the Almighty. Therefore shall hands be faint, and every man's heart shall melt; And they shall be afraid; pangs and sorrows shall take hold of them; they shall be in pain as a woman that travaileth. (Isaiah 13:6–8)

When the dour ascetic known as John the Baptist made his appearance—"the voice of one crying in the wilderness, Prepare ye the way of the Lord, make his paths straight," calling on all Judea to repent and be cleansed in the waters of the Jordan—it was as one in the same fierce succession. During a time of political volatility within the Roman Empire, of threatened insurrection and growing factionalism among the Jews themselves, references to the day of the Lord were frequent. Since the desecration of the Temple, there had been a tendency to regard the enemies of Israel (rather than her own backsliding) as the real target of the wrath to come. For the strictly pious sect know as the Pharisees—among whom Paul had himself been prominent—the day of the Lord meant, in fact, the end of the world.

This kind of thinking was not altogether new. A tradition of apocalyptic writing went back at least two hundred years, to an anonymous Hebrew work which we know as the Book of Daniel. Along with predicting the end of time, it contains this declaration: "And many of those who sleep in the dust of the earth shall awake, some to everlasting life, and some to everlasting shame and contempt." The books of the law and the prophets had said little hitherto concerning the fate of the individual soul. But such apocalyptic forecasts would have been familiar to believing Jews and especially to the Pharisees, who looked for the coming of the Messiah, the Chosen One, to usher in a new age and reign forever. In the writings of Saint Paul, the effect of such thinking is unmistakable. The first Epistle to the Thessalonians has an echo of Isaiah:

For you yourselves know well that the day of the Lord will come like a thief in the night. When people say, "There is peace and security," then sudden destruction will come upon them as travail comes upon a woman with child; and there will be no escape. (5: 2–3)

It has also an echo of the Book of Daniel:

For the Lord himself will descend from heaven with a cry of command, with the archangel's call, and with the sound of the trumpet of God. And the dead in Christ shall rise first; then we who are alive, who are left, shall be caught up together with them in the cloud to meet the Lord in the air: and so we shall always be with the Lord. (4: 16–17)

This, for churchgoers of every sect and persuasion, is the central message of Paul's first Epistle to the Thessalonians. I can't remember now when I first heard it in so many biblical words; but I had been acquainted with it by way of a hymn that was a regular part of the opening exercises at Sunday school. Since I haven't heard it sung, or so much as seen it in print, for more than half a century, it evokes for me the damp of the church basement in which the youngest of us were corralled, while the adult Bible classes met upstairs. I hear the pumping wheeze of the reed organ, with its rows of buttons for adjusting the stops, as we sang the refrain:

When He *com*-eth, when He *com*-eth *to* make up His *jew*-els,
All the *pure* ones, all the *bright* ones, *His* loved *and* His
own . . . .

"Jew-ulls," was the way I still hear it; and "love *dan*dy zone." For sheer inanity there can't have been anything to surpass it before the advent of the sung commercial. Not a few of the hymns I remember best provided a foretaste of the commercial's rollicking glibness:

Oh, Beulah Land, *Sweet* Beulah Land,
As *on* thy highest mount I stand,

> I look away across the sea
> Where mansions are prepared for me . . . .

Such rollicking is hard to resist, and I entered in as lustily as anyone else. All the same, it sounded to me like a travesty of something I didn't believe a word of. What I did believe, crassly and from an early age, was that out in the real world, religion—i.e., having to go to church—was already obsolete. And in fact (I am not trying to excuse myself here) the little country church where I wriggled through several hundred mornings of Sunday school followed by preaching, praying, and the singing of hymns, was to a degree benighted. The community had been settled by members of the Society of Friends (or Quakers, as they didn't mind calling themselves), who in the welter of late-nineteenth-century evangelism had lost track of precisely who they were, or had been: they no longer sat in silence to await the promptings of the Inner Light but relied on a pastor, as well as a choir, to guide them. They omitted baptism and would have bridled still more at the idea of Communion, even when the wine was only grape juice; but in what mattered they differed hardly at all from any evangelical denomination.

What to the evangelical denominations mattered above all, and to the practical exclusion of very much else, was of course the Second Coming. Not that any such expression is to be found in the Epistles of Saint Paul. The one he did use, the one from which so enormous a freight of doctrine now depends, is the Greek word *parousia.* Deriving from the verb *pareinai,* "to be present," it has the pristine meaning of a presence, a being-there, and by extension came to denote an arrival, a visit, an appearance—or, as the King James Bible has it, a Coming. Unmodified, it is a word the Apostle used over and over. "For what is our hope or joy or crown of boasting before our Lord Jesus Christ at his coming?" he wrote to the Thessalonians. And again, "that he may establish your hearts unblamable in holiness before our God and Father, at the coming of our Lord Jesus Christ"—and yet again, "we who are alive, who are left until the coming of the Lord." By the time of the second Epistle to the Thessalonians—and concerning just when Paul wrote it, or indeed whether he or someone else is the author, scholars disagree—there had begun to be confusion and uncertainty, such as have not abated from that day to this:

> Now concerning the coming of our Lord Jesus Christ and our assembling to meet him, we beg you, brethren, not to be quickly shaken in mind or excited, either by spirit or by word, or by letter purporting to be from us, to the effect that the day of the Lord has come. (2: 1–2)

Drawing repeatedly on the imagery of the Old Testament—"mighty angels in flaming fire, inflicting vengeance upon those who do not know God and upon those who do not obey the gospel of our Lord Jesus"—the letter proceeds to outline what had become, among the Jews, a familiar apocalyptic scenario:

> Let no one deceive you in any way, for his day will not come unless the rebellion comes first, and the man of lawlessness is revealed, the son of perdition, who opposes and exalts himself against every so-called god or object of worship, so that he takes his seat in the temple of God, proclaiming himself to be God. (2:3–4)

If the Thessalonians, those exemplary converts from paganism, could so easily be deluded into supposing that the advent of the Chosen One had, in some invisible and secret fashion, already occurred, what hope is there for any of the rest of us? Given *their* confusion, the casuistries, the contortions, the outright monstrosities that have been brought forth in the name and under the rubric of eschatology—the study of last things—are hardly a cause for wonder. For those who withstood the temptation to think in wholly incorporeal terms, as the Gnostics were condemned for doing, there was nothing left to do but wait.

In the rural community where I grew up, the old silent waiting for the still small voice, for that which is of God in every man, as the old Quakers had put it, amounted perhaps to a homespun sort of Gnosticism. But it had been superseded. The waiting now was for something noisier, for the upheaval that would signal that the Second Coming was at hand. I remember hearing the son of perdition, the expected Antichrist, equated with Adolf Hitler. If so, the world had not long to wait. The jewels must be gathered up, the sinners called to repentance. There must be, in words I remember hearing from the pulpit, Sunday after Sunday, a Revival.

Of that particular Revival, if it can be said to have occurred, I was never a witness. The nearest I came to it was a mildly prurient report from the "hired girl" with whom I shared a room, of indignities she had witnessed at an evening's call for sinners to come forward. From somewhere or other I had snobbishly absorbed a belief that to be Saved in so public a manner was for those who Didn't Know Any Better, and thus of no consequence. Otherwise, the evangelical note was a longwinded nostalgic drone, or else a form of teasing:

> "Tell me something. Are you a Bryl-Creem Christian? A little dab'll do ya? Are you an Alka-Seltzer Baptist? Put him in the water and he'll fizz for half a minute? Are you a C & E Christian—Christmas and Easter?"
>
> And so on with On and Off, Hot and Cold, Lost and Found, Mini and Maxi, Before and After, Sweet and Low, Short and Sweet, Brown and Serve. The attendant bouquet of Gethsemane Christians smile and murmur their laughter at one another, and Kingsley finishes the series with an upbeat appreciation.
>
> "With all your faults and blemishes, I contend that you are the best crowd. God's crowd is the in-crowd, the only crowd that will make it in heaven."

Thus Rebecca Hill in *Blue Rise*, a novel set in rural Mississippi, but with so exact an ear that it transcends locality. The diction of evangelism in the second millennium of waiting is nothing if not strenuously up to date.

> Just think of it . . . in the flash of a second every living believer on earth will be gone. Suddenly, without warning, only unbelievers will be populating planet earth. . . .
>
> We will suddenly one day just blast off into space. Faster than the eye of the unbeliever can perceive, every living be-

liever on earth will disappear. The world will probably hear a great sonic boom from all our transformed immortal bodies cracking the sound barrier. But the rest will be a mystery.

Thus *The Rapture* by Hal Lindsey, an author of note (his first book, *The Late Great Planet Earth*, is reported to have sold eighteen million copies), as well as a pastor and broadcast evangelist. Nor is this quite all. As the apocalyptic scenario is fulfilled, he tells us,

> The whole world will probably see this by satellite television. We now have the technical ability to fulfill what is predicted, "And those from the peoples and tribes and tongues and nations will look at their dead bodies for three days and a half, and will not permit their dead bodies to be laid in a tomb." (Revelation 11:9)

As Susan Sontag has observed, reality bifurcates: there is the event and there is the image of the event.

For Hal Lindsey himself, the strategy meanwhile has been to "gain a combat knowledge of the Bible in order to be able to face the perilous times that precede the Tribulation. It motivates me," he declares, "to win as many to Christ as possible before it's too late. I want to take as many with me as I can."

That is one extreme—an alarming one, surely, for anyone less confident than the Reverend Mr. Lindsey. It is to his credit that he evinces concern for the fate of the people of Israel. "Most believe," he says—evidently referring to other fundamentalist spokesmen—"that [a] place of protection for believing Israel will be the ancient fortress city of Petra," in southern Jordan—though given its history of sudden flooding, among other drawbacks, one wonders.

The opposite extreme, among those disposed to consider the matter at all, is less stark but more problematic. It entails an admission, such as only the most dogmatic of literalists can fail to be troubled by:

> With each passing generation, the person of Christ became more absent, more tenuous. To counteract the withdrawal of the historical Christ, believers had the words of Christ concern-

ing the Spirit and the Second Coming: the present and the future promises. . . . The experience of the Spirit is necessarily mystical and enthusiastic by nature (in enthusiasm's original sense of being possessed by a god). . . . The Second Coming is equally problematic as a focus for belief. Its promise is dependent on Christ's words, which are in themselves dependent on the certainty or uncertainty of the written text, their inseparable matrix.

Thus Anthony Kemp in *The Estrangement of the Past*, which as a work in progress has been of great help to my own thinking. The problem is elaborated in a book called *The First Coming* where Thomas Sheehan, a professor of philosophy at Loyola University in Chicago, examines what he calls the "Jesus-Movement's" early history:

The problem was not that the disciples frequently met resistance from the religious establishment: That, in fact, was grist for their mill. . . . The serious problem, rather, was the lengthening of the supposedly brief interval between Jesus' hidden vindication at his death and his public reappearance in glory. Not only was the parousia being progressively delayed, but within thirty years of Jesus' death the founders of the eschatological movement within Judaism would begin dying off, with no return of Jesus yet in sight. (Pp. 192–93)

Once Professor Sheehan has stripped back the layers of dogmatic accretion from the slight and brittle fabric of historicity, there is not much that can be said with certitude. However, I believe that something can—otherwise this look at what Saint Paul wrote will have been an empty exercise.

As a matter of historicity, Paul was himself a latecomer. He had never met the man Jesus. He did not claim to have done so, only that "as to one untimely born, He appeared also to me." Here, again, is Professor Sheehan on that event:

Paul hears a voice but *sees nothing*. In fact he is rendered temporarily blind by "a light from heaven, brighter than the sun" (Acts 26:13; cf. 9:3, 22:6). Even more important, when Paul himself described his experience some fifteen years after it happened, he called it not a vision but more neutrally an apocalyptic "revelation" (apokalypsis, Galatians 1:12). (P. 116)

Though it happened to a saint of the church, an experience of this sort is not beyond the ken of ordinary humanity. Such experiences are perhaps not uncommon. They can be, and frequently are, reduced to clinical terms—which in no way, as William James was at pains to demonstrate, invalidates the effect, the forces that may have been set in motion. For Saint Paul himself, zealous opposition had prepared the way for the reversal, the conversion of energies that empowered him to become a founder, if not indeed sole inventor, of what we call Christianity. Many of us, in our own minor fashion, have experienced some such conversion of energies. For me, the way had been prepared by exposure to music and painting, as well as to the writing of the likes of Dante, Donne, Hopkins, and (I dare say) T. S. Eliot. Of the immediate particulars, I recall mainly that on a Sunday afternoon I had wandered into the museum familiarly known as The Cloisters, where in the midst of listening to a piped-in motet, for an unasked-for moment all habitual concerns gave way to a serenity so perfect that it amounted to a lapse of consciousness—or perhaps it is clinically more accurate to speak of a lapse so complete that it amounted to perfect serenity. The event was so totally unasked-for, and the lapse so infinitesimal, that it passed almost unnoticed. It was only later, in astonished retrospect, that I found a word for what by then felt like an intervening flood. The word was Grace. Though nothing from that day to this has caused me to gainsay it, the flood soon had me spinning out of control. I was about to be a famous poet, perhaps even the founder of a new religion. Elation became mania, which acquired by degrees the complexion of terror. The term I found for my condition now was Mortal Sin. Outside of my private turmoil, it happened to be Holy Week. I found myself in church; there seemed literally nowhere else to go. And having gone in, I stayed in. With the enthusiasm of the typical convert, I was now a churchgoer.

While the enthusiasm was at its flood, I had no doctrinal worries. I believed whatever I was asked to believe. The flood stage passed; years passed, and I began to discover just how rigidly callous a preserve I had wandered into. The trouble, finally and above all, was its callousness toward the Jews. What goes on in an Anglo-Catholic house of worship may be in better taste than in most others. The music at any rate can be gorgeous, and was one reason I gravitated there. But when it comes to the people of Israel, the fundamentalist bodies are more respectful. Perhaps T. S. Eliot was never really an anti-Semite—the record is muddled, as records tend to be—but polite Anglicanism unmistakably harbors the chill of bigotry; and so, it would seem, does the entire institutional structure that is the Church.

The flaw is there, like the flaw in Henry James's allegorical golden bowl, before the sumptuous gift can be offered: the assurance, that is, that the Chosen One would come to make up his jewels—Saint Paul declaring, early in his first Epistle to the Thessalonians, "for you suffered the same things from your own countrymen as they did from the Jews, who killed both the Lord Jesus and the prophets." To whatever in the way of extenuation and qualification this statement, by a man who was himself a Jew, may lend itself, the effect in practice is by now incalculable.

From the Good Friday liturgy, in which for years I was an enthusiastic participant, Pontius Pilate emerges as rather a nice man, at least by comparison with the yelling mob who are the Jews personified. Not Pilate's fault, according to the liturgy. The historical record, as bluntly set forth by Thomas Sheehan, is otherwise:

> Pontius Pilate . . . had arrived in Palestine in the Roman year 779 (26 c.e.). . . . Today he would probably, and correctly, be called an anti-Semite. His main jobs were to collect taxes and keep the public order as he put in his time in the provinces, awaiting a better assignment; but from the moment he arrived in the country he seemed never to miss a chance to offend pious Jews and in more than one instance to threaten and murder them. . . . In any case, whatever Pilate's reasons for deciding to have Jesus put to death, it is not true that the Jewish crowds shouted out that Jesus should be crucified (Mark 15:12ff.) or that they took his blood upon themselves

and their children (Matthew 27:25). Nor did the high priest tell the prefect "We have no king but Caesar" (John 19:15). These sentences, which were later written into the accounts of Jesus' passion, are the products of a bitter polemic between early Christianity and Judaism and have helped to cause the horrors of two millennia of anti-Semitism. (Pp. 55, 87)

There remains to note a terse report from the Annals of Tacitus, written around A.D. 114, that a man named Christ was put to death by Pontius Pilate during the reign of Tiberius.

This record notwithstanding, most churchgoers continue to believe what they absorbed at an early age: the Jews did it, or if the Romans did it, it was because the Jews wanted them to. Can so longstanding a calumny be extirpated? At this late date, there are theologians at work. Here is one, Lloyd Gaston, quoting the words of another:

> Rosemary Ruether has posed in all its sharpness what must surely be *the* theological question for Christians in our generation: "Possibly anti-Judaism is too deeply embedded in the foundations of Christianity to be rooted out entirely without destroying the whole structure." It may be that the church will survive if we fail to deal adequately with that question, but more serious is the question whether the church ought to survive. (*Paul and the Torah*, p. 15)

All this is somewhat grimmer than anything I quite expected when I set out to consider the earliest known document to mention the name of Jesus of Nazareth. Who was he? A Jew with no plans to found a new religion, who simply *was* what he proclaimed—that the Kingdom of Heaven is here and now. I think of modern Thessalonica, where the authentic residues of a Byzantine past amount to little more than a glimmer of mosaic, defaced, covered over and uncovered, further defacement being the price of salvaging anything at all.

Some such traces persist of a historical person, a blithe, severe, and luminous exemplar whom neither the accretions of time nor the effort to dislodge them can quite obliterate. What, if anything, those traces may have to do with the kind of experience I have described—with those vivid energies rushing in from beyond one's own resources—I am not so foolhardy as to attempt even a guess. The conviction flowing from such an experience, that what is most real is the incorporeal, is borne out by what physicists tell us of the material universe. Yet such a conviction has inevitably to contend with an overbearing weight of evidence to the contrary. The accretions of history, of its folly and turpitude, stare us down. Any effort to return that stare, with all one's sympathies in place, would be next to intolerable. We inhabit a ruin of embattled certitudes, an incarceration of error fossilized, of an injustice so appalling that for any response at all there seems nowhere to turn but to the Hebrew prophets. With such a condition, humankind can deal only in very small doses: T. S. Eliot was right about that. One can concur and at the same time be persuaded, with another Christian poet, that nevertheless "there lives the dearest freshness deep down things." For all its institutional horrors, the strength of Christianity remains that it is founded on a paradox: whatever we know of incorporeal reality is to date inseparable from the channels that received it. The long wait continues for the power of the incorporeal to manifest itself in one final dogmatic showdown. But in what is discernible of the life and teachings of Jesus himself, the incorporeal, in all its freshness, is here and now.

SOURCES

The Writings of St. Paul: Annotated Text and Criticism, edited by Wayne A. Meeks. New York: Norton, 1972.

The New Testament of Our Lord and Saviour Jesus Christ, edited by Thomas M. Lindsay. London and New York: Everyman, 1907.

Letters to Young Churches: A Translation of the New Testament Epistles, by J. B. Phillips. New York: Macmillan, 1958.

Blue Rise, by Rebecca Hill. New York: Penguin, 1984.

The Rapture: Truth or Consequences, by Hal Lindsey. New York: Bantam, 1983, 1985.

The Estrangement of the Past, by Anthony Kemp. New York: Oxford University Press, 1990.

The First Coming: How the Kingdom of God Became Christianity, by Thomas Sheehan. New York: Random House, 1986.

Paul and the Torah, by Lloyd Gaston. Vancouver: University of British Columbia Press, 1987.

"AIDS and Its Metaphors," by Susan Sontag. *New York Review of Books,* October 27, 1988.

The Maverick Career of
Thomas McGrath

Thomas McGrath was born in 1916, a year before Robert
Lowell—a poet with whom one might suppose (wrongly) that
he had nothing in common. Both of McGrath's grandfathers
were Irish immigrant homesteaders on the plains of North
Dakota. His father, who had been a lumberjack and worked
on the railroad before settling down as a farmer, was self-
educated, a born storyteller, and an instinctive radical: in 1940
he voted Communist. Growing up during the Depression in a
part of the country where strikes by agricultural laborers were
frequent, and where a grass-roots left-wing movement, the
Nonpartisan League, flourished as nowhere else, the young
Tom McGrath read everything he could lay his hands on—
and though books were not easy to come by, they included
such things as *Ulysses, Swann's Way,* and the Modern Library
anthology of modern poetry.

By the summer of 1938, as he would later recall, McGrath
had begun writing poetry of his own. A year later he graduated
from the University of North Dakota and won a Rhodes scholar-
ship. Because of the war in Europe and his own circumstances,
he did not go to Oxford until 1947. In the meantime he wound
up in Baton Rouge, on a graduate scholarship from Louisiana
State. He did not meet Robert Lowell, who arrived there a year
later, and he may or may not have known the late Robert Penn
Warren; but the latter's colleague and coauthor Cleanth

Adapted from a review originally published in the *Nation,* November
6, 1989. Reprinted by permission.

Brooks became his friend and mentor, notwithstanding a principled opposition—Southern agrarian versus Northern farm boy who had already cast his lot with the Communists. Joining the CP might still be fashionable in some quarters; but Tom McGrath stayed in, or anyhow stayed "red," long after it was comfortable or even safe.

He had a year at Oxford, and had been teaching for three years at Los Angeles State College when the House Un-American Affairs Committee caught up with him. Called on to testify about "Communist activities in the educational and motion picture fields," he made a statement that was unique in the reason it offered for not cooperating; he might have been talking back to Jesse Helms, and not an unremembered successor to Martin Dies:

> As a poet I must refuse to cooperate with the committee on what I can only call esthetic grounds. The view of life which we receive through the great works of art is a privileged one—it is a view of life according to probability or necessity, not subject to the chance and accident of our real world and therefore in a sense truer than the life we see lived all around us. . . .
>
> As a teacher, my first responsibility is to my students. To cooperate with this committee would be to set for them an example of accommodation to forces which can only have, as their end effect, the destruction of education itself. . . . I am proud to say that a great majority of my students . . . do not want me to accommodate myself to this committee. In a certain sense, I have no choice in the matter. . . .

There were student protests when he seemed about to lose his job; but he lost it anyhow, and found himself on an academic blacklist. Eventually he was invited back to North Dakota, and later across the border to Minnesota, to teach; but for a decade or so he made a fly-by-night sort of living, writing filmstrips and pulp fiction, working in factories—whatever he could find in the way of menial labor. The real irony here is that as a deep-dyed Marxist, but above all a nonconformist, McGrath had gone on writing poetry that was too extreme—too "bitter" is the word they used—for the ruling literati of the CP. In a letter to a longtime friend, the noted British

Socialist E. P. Thompson, he observed: "Unless you versify *Daily Worker* editorials in degenerate Whitmanesque, you're apt to seem like a formalist, and anything that is not a cliché is examined to see whether it might be a political heresy."

In 1949, a year or so before this letter was written, a collection of McGrath's poems, *Longshot O'Leary's Garland of Practical Poesie*, had been brought out by International Publishers, the publishing arm of the Communist Party. There would be no more books of his under that imprint. Early in 1949, reports appeared in the newspapers concerning a possible Soviet spy ring, and in connection with a mention of the writer Agnes Smedley, a pair of FBI agents turned up at Yaddo, the writers' and artists' colony in upstate New York. Robert Lowell happened to be there at the time, and there are accounts by Alfred Kazin and others of the unpleasantness that ensued. Politically, Lowell and McGrath were just then at opposite poles. Whereas Lowell, reacting against his New England upbringing, had become a Roman Catholic convert, McGrath had been brought up in a household that was nominally Catholic. The references one finds in his work to the Church of Rome are generally sardonic, in contrast to the intensely devotional coloring of, say, "The Quaker Graveyard in Nantucket"; in fact, McGrath has an account of a first confession, toward the end of his *Letter to an Imaginary Friend*, that is pure *buffo*.

But it's easy to make too much of this, even if Lowell hadn't left the Roman church before long. Polar extremes of attitude have a way of converging; and in a more fundamental way, two poets who happened to be in ideological opposition seem to have been driven by an almost identical loathing for the prevalent culture.

As young poets, one thing the two had in common was an admiration for Hart Crane. Lowell once spoke of Crane as being "at the center of things" in his own time—a remark I find baffling. The center of things? Hart Crane, son of a candy manufacturer in Garrettsville, Ohio, and a misfit from the day he was born? It's true that nobody ever seems to have thought of him as a regional poet, any more than Robert Lowell was thought to be one because he was born in Massachusetts. Or than T. S. Eliot, born in St. Louis, Missouri, or Ezra Pound, born in Hailey, Idaho, are thought of as regional poets. All were to a greater or lesser degree alienated from their places of birth. As W. H. Auden, an expatriate from the opposite direction, observed in connection with that quintessential expatriate Henry James, "It is sometimes necessary for sons to leave the family hearth; it may well be necessary at least for intellectuals to leave their country as it is for children to leave their homes, not to get away from them, but to re-create them." There may be the germ of an explanation here for why writers tagged as regional tend, when they're noticed at all, to be thought of as second-class citizens in the not at all democratic republic of letters. This would appear to be what happened to Thomas McGrath. It wasn't simply a matter of being from North Dakota. Besides his year at Oxford, he has spent time in Greece and Portugal, not to mention New York and Los Angeles. But I myself was not aware of his work until an evening a few years ago, when I heard him read from it to a gathering in Grand Forks. He was obviously well known to many in the audience, and perhaps that is why I ticked him off as a "regional figure." He looked old and ill, and sounded bitter. I mention all this, in some embarrassment, because it occurs to me that the phenomenon of inattention may have a larger part in literary reputation, or lack of it, than is generally admitted.

As a judge in a competition you are obliged to try to make up for such lapses of attention; and that is what Robert Shaw, Richard Kenney, and I found ourselves doing when we chose Thomas McGrath's *Selected Poems 1938–1988* for the 1989 Lenore Marshall Award. The choice was unanimous and was arrived at without prolonged difficulty once we had resigned ourselves to the agony of having to choose at all among numerous works of distinction, freshness, or endearingly outright outlandishness, if not all three.

We were aware, as judges, that McGrath's evident gifts had not gone unrecognized. The Guggenheim Foundation, the National Endowment for the Arts, and those with the Amy Lowell Travelling Fellowship in their gift, among others, had all favored him with grants. But the kind of critical attention that gets a poet into the mainstream anthologies had still not come his way.

Some readers coming upon his work for the first time must have wondered why. A sober and temperate effort to provide an answer is to be found in *The Revolutionary Poet in the United States*, a collection of essays edited by Frederick Stern (University of Missouri Press, 1988). Such are the vagaries of publishing and reviewing, not to speak of sheer inattention, that neither I nor my fellow judges had previously laid eyes on McGrath's *Letter to an Imaginary Friend*. Begun at a low moment in the 1950s, it had by 1984, when he pronounced it complete, grown to epic length—a difficulty in itself, so far as publishers are concerned. Nevertheless, beginning in 1962, part by part it found its way into print (parts 1 and 2 under the imprint of the Swallow Press, parts 3 and 4 of Copper Canyon). Repairing the omission in my own reading, I found the *Letter* to be by turns fierce, somber, rollicking, and outrageous—a simmering *olla podrida* of an epic, from which there is the urge at moments, perhaps, to turn away. Only one doesn't; there is also an urge to stick around even when the party appears to be getting out of hand.

The *Selected Poems 1938–1988* (Copper Canyon) is by comparison sedate, though it does have its extravagances. Sam Hamill's introduction may mislead the unwary into supposing that the *Letter* is not represented at all. Happily, however, there is some overlap, since it could be said (and has been, as the poet himself admits) that his entire work adds up to "only one poem throughout." This is not to be taken quite literally. The selection includes a number of poems no bigger than a haiku and just as autonomous.

> The long wound of the summer—
> Stitched
> by cicadas

is one example.

> Through the fog
> The gulls
> Carry the sea
> Inland

is another. But it is also true, as it was true of Wordsworth, say, or Whitman, that the work as a whole does leave one with the sense of something single, however large, loose, fragmentary, and indeed at times disorderly. The "neatness of finish" exemplified by Marianne Moore (though she had her own sly reservations on that score) is by no means absent. A fondness for the well-turned stanza is evident from beginning to end, as well as a longer, looser cadence that seems to settle most naturally into a six-beat line.

If one assumes, however, an affinity with Whitman, or with Sandburg, that assumption is soon confounded: to begin with, at least, McGrath has said he didn't much care for either one. Among early likes he has mentioned Conrad Aiken and Robinson Jeffers, along with Hart Crane. When it comes to outright borrowing—from Eliot, Blake, Keats, Yeats, Stevens, Marvell, Donne, Rilke, Saint Francis—he is unabashed. The strongest unacknowledged influence would seem to be that of W. H. Auden. The adjectives, the alliteration, the feeling for topography, are all at any rate to be found in an early poem such as "Up the Dark Valley." Reticence, economy, and neatness on the page are also to be found in such later poems as the balladlike "Remembering the Children of Auschwitz":

And all seemed perfectly proper:
The little house was covered
With barbwire and marzipan;
And the Witch was there; and the Oven.

Imitation conscious or unconscious, pastiche, the trying on of masks, may turn out to be the refuge of whoever grows up alienated. It was true of Eliot and Pound, who between them reinvented poetry as a thing of rags and patches. If the *Selected Poems* of Thomas McGrath contains its share of pastiche, of borrowings and unconscious echoes, no one should be surprised. The very title of his *Letter to an Imaginary Friend* is symptomatic of his own isolation:

Stood in the north Forty,
With no tradition to warm me, demanding a name,
Needing a word for the Now . . .

Exile begins early in my country
Though the commune of gentle wood choppers be never so
    wide and warm.

In the absence of any native tradition, there may be a trying
on of masks and manners, but also a recklessness as all these
are flung aside, and what opens is a welter of possibilities.

And the Pheasant leaped out of the tenement of the corn like
    a burglar taken
In flagrante delicto with a cry like an angry bedspring
(Part silver, part bronze, part wind chime and part pure galva-
    nized iron:
A gateless gate opening on hinges never been oiled
By a single Koan)—*leaped!* showing his colors, those jewels
Blazing around his neck, in a hellish and helicopterish
Blur and burr of feathers: indignant bandido and banshee!

This, from part 3 of the *Letter,* does not appear in the *Selected
Poems,* though other passages from it do recur there: "Praises,"
a succulent catalog of vegetable "modes and virtues," is one.
How, it may be asked, can such exuberance consort with the ire
of a lifelong Marxist? Uneasily: that much may perhaps be said,
though in the end the ire is not merely polemical, but is fed by
the same deep sources as the poetry itself.

One of those sources, for the poet in question, is the experi-
ence of work. No poet, I think, since Whitman has written so
obsessively of physical labor as McGrath has done—though in
an altered and more elegiac tone:

The bunched cooperative labor of poor stiffs in the cold.
All dead now: that kind of working. Only
The trees the same: cottonwood, chokecherry; elm; ash;
Oak and box elder.
                    Every man on his own.

                                                    It's here
      Someplace
                  all went wrong.
                                      For work alone is play
      Or slavery.
                  Went wrong somewhere.

The ire, Marxist or not, that can issue in such sorrow is part of
the poet's calling—to brace and bring to its senses what the
times have all but narcotized.

John Berryman: The Poet as a Self-Made American

The poet out of control—drunken, skirt-chasing, self-destructive if not an outright suicide—has amounted to an icon since Dylan Thomas first careened into the news. His notoriety may have had something vicarious about it, and thus have been peculiar to the 1950s; but if so, an alarming number of his American contemporaries were all too soon to undo themselves likewise. After not only Thomas, but also Delmore Schwartz, Theodore Roethke, and Randall Jarrell had all gone to their untimely deaths, Robert Lowell would write of how John Berryman "in his mad way keeps talking about something evil stalking us poets."

Berryman had envisioned Ezra Pound as "anxious to find out *what has gone wrong,* with money and government, that has produced our situation for the Poet." For Berryman himself, a great deal had been almost mythically wrong since his twelfth year, when the presumed suicide of his actual father, John Allyn Smith, was quickly followed by his mother's marriage to the man who had been her lover and whose surname the boy now assumed. A fragile sense of his own identity would have been unsurprising in one less imaginative than the young John Berryman. That he often behaved like a textbook case of hysteria and infantile regression is thus explicable, however tiresome. That he could also be generous and thoughtful is attested by many witnesses. He dazzled countless young women—three of whom, each exceptional

Originally published in the *Boston Sunday Globe,* February 4, 1990.

in her own right, put up bravely with being married to him. That he was a writer above all is inseparable from both the best and the worst about him. Besides a dozen books, he left an intriguing mass of unpublished papers. No poet since Coleridge, it would seem, was so compulsive a diarist—and indeed it is Coleridge, rather than any contemporary, whom John Berryman the talkative addict most resembles. But whereas Coleridge, his intake of laudanum under control, managed to settle down and go on talking, Berryman found no way out other than the one he took when he leaped from a bridge at the age of fifty-seven. The tragedy of the confirmed alcoholic was poignantly stated by a friend and colleague who "concluded that the only John one could love was a John with 2 or 3 drinks in him, no more & no less, & such a John could not exist."

What value is there in following the ups and downs of such a history? More than once during six years of living day and night (as he tells us) with Berryman's voluminous legacy, Paul Mariani must have asked himself that question. Eileen Simpson, in a memoir of great charm and authority, had given a first-hand version; John Haffenden had made a beginning at tackling the diaries, though what he presented was mainly the man other people had known. Paul Mariani's concern was with the man himself—the harrowings of the life within, as recorded but still largely untranscribed. He had a hunch, moreover, that Berryman's importance as a poet was greater than had been supposed. After writing a life of William Carlos Williams, he would lend his own imagination to a different, even a contrary force, and be educated accordingly.

"He has not been an easy master, Mr. Berryman," the biographer-pupil declares, his struggle finally over. That it was a struggle, a veritable tar baby of a project—a tar baby tricked out in the long gray beard and glittering eye of the Ancient Mariner—is evident from the thrashings of a syntax full of clots and abrasions, the tautologies of sheer exhaustion. That Mr. Mariani, himself a poet, is capable of felicitous prose is evident from his preface to *Dream Song: The Life of John Berryman* (Morrow, 1990). The constraints of space are part of the trouble: he acknowledges the help of his editor in reducing a 1,250-page text to one-half that length. He could have used more help than he got: aside from the uncushioned jolts and elisions, there is a speckling of error (names misspelled, confusion over the Volstead Act) that, though of no real consequence, can distract a reader.

This reader came away nevertheless with a final respect for the biographer's steadiness of purpose and clarity of insight. Vexed though his sympathies have been he refrains from passing moral judgment—as any reader will be tempted to do several times on a single page—on the character of his subject.

The character of any of us is to some degree an invention, hitched to an armature of what can't be altered. If Berryman returned from a stay in England with a set of affectations that Mark Van Doren, kindest of mentors, found insufferable, should anyone be surprised? Berryman's own insufferable mother had changed her Christian name (from Martha to Jill Angel) and liked to think she could pass as her son's sister. One may wince; but consider the case of Thomas Stearns Eliot, who remade himself in the image of a London clubman, who got away with it and then some. The far more mercurial Berryman was in fact so driven—by anxiety, by nightmares, by a moiling windbag of ambitions, of things not done, possibilities unrealized—that the process of defining himself could hardly even begin.

"No! I am not Prince Hamlet, nor was meant to be," sighed Eliot in the earlier guise of J. Alfred Prufrock. Berryman more than halfway believed he *was* Hamlet. Lecturing on the subject at Princeton, he set a trap to catch his mother's guilty conscience, if she had one. In a farcical countermove, his mother arrived late, all eyes upon her as she swept to her place in the front row. Upstaged, Berryman managed to postpone flying into a tantrum until the lecture was over. As his life proceeded, the infant that lives on in all of us came more and more to dominate everything he did, aside from teaching—at which he was eerily successful—and, of course, writing.

Mastery of his craft came late. When his *77 Dream Songs* won the Pulitzer Prize in 1965, the form he had gradually devised to harness the chaos within himself celebrated, in effect, the tenth birthday of Henry, the dream-protagonist for whom Berryman is most likely to be remembered. Much of his earlier poetry had been a solemn imitation of Yeats. The *Homage to Mistress Bradstreet* is grueling, cryptic, and charmless. But the Dream Songs not only had a new and crazy charm, they were also funny. In the paranoid and cagily gibbering Henry, Berryman had brought on a new clown, the comic peer of Prufrock and of Samuel Beckett's Vladimir and Estragon, to inhabit the wasteland that was the consciousness of the twentieth century.

> Henry under construction was Henry indeed:
> gigantic cranes faltered under the load . . .

To the end of Berryman's life, the construction went on: the last of the Dream Songs was written just two days before his suicide.

During a drunken interview a year before, Paul Mariani tells us, Berryman described himself as "a medium for the larger forces going on around him, a sort of national sounding board." And perhaps there was some truth in this, after all. His own generation had coincided with the gathering evidence that though the country of the self-made had won a war, it could not run the world. Its poets, in their various uneasy ways, were the first to register what nobody wanted or knew how to think about. The Dream Songs, Berryman declared, were about him and his friends (among them these same poets) and God.

More and more, the record of Berryman's last months is about God. Awake and sober in a Hartford hotel room between 1:15 and 2:15 A.M., as he compulsively noted, on a day in May six months before he died, he set down in the form of a poem, "The Facts & Issues," the tergiversations of one who has been vouchsafed a mystical experience, only to turn it into a tantrum of refusal:

> I am so happy I could scream!
> It's *enough!* I can't BEAR ANY MORE.
> *Let this be it.* I've *had* it. I can't wait.

Though the speaker is not Henry, and the poem is not funny, it does suggest something about Henry as a self-made creature— and perhaps about what has gone wrong in the country of the self-made. Asked in yet another interview "whether or not the artist had a responsibility to affirm something finally, Berryman answered no. How else, he added, could one explain someone like Beckett, who had a mind so dark it made one wonder 'if the Renaissance ever really took place.' "

Whatever Berryman meant by this, it is instructive to compare the jazzy, pseudo-blackface irreverence of Henry at his funniest with Beckett's laconic, bowler-hatted tramps. For them, the old figures of authority had vanished. Yet unlike Henry, who seems to have had something to do with God, the benighted Vladimir and Estragon, when last seen, were still managing to wait.

Stevie Smith: The Desolation
of the Ordinary

The fame of Stevie Smith has been sporadic but persistent. It began in 1936, when her *Novel on Yellow Paper* had an immediate celebrity. In her last years she became a star of the poetry-reading circuit, sharing the stage with Robert Lowell and drawing warmer applause (we are told) than W. H. Auden. But in between, her second and third novels received little attention, and her poems had trouble finding a publisher. Since her death in 1971, not only the poems but all three of her novels have been reissued, and she is now the subject of (in addition to Glenda Jackson's well-known stage and screen portrayal) not one but two biographies.

"Two biographies! How Stevie, who had enjoyed her late fame so very much, would have laughed!" is the comment of Jack Barbera and William McBrien at the end of *Stevie*, published here in 1987. At the book's beginning, a courteous pair of notes made it clear that the authorized biography was till to come.

And here it is, complete with an equally civil bow by its author (who has books on Vanessa Bell and Roger Fry to her credit) in the direction of her predecessors. In no way a counter-biography but rather one whose intent is to build on, refine, and clarify what has gone before, Frances Spaulding's *Stevie Smith* (Norton, 1989) is somewhat more closely textured and formally more coherent. The opening, on the subject's family background in the port city of Hull, where she lived

---

Originally published in the *Boston Sunday Globe*, May 28, 1989.

until she was three, and the touching chapter on her final illness, are especially admirable. Some fresh material has come to light as people who had known Stevie Smith were tracked down and interviewed. The portrait that emerges is of a profoundly troubled, troublesome, but on the whole appealing character.

At one level, certainly, she does not come off well. She was forever giving offense—much of it, in the manner of D. H. Lawrence, to those who had befriended her. But nobody was exempt. Shortly after the formal investiture of the current Prince of Wales in July, 1969, she was heard to declaim in the midst of a swimming party:

> We have given the Welsh a most *awfully*
> Nice day out
> And now we never want to hear from them again
> For *years,* and *years,* and *years,*
> And never at all
> In *Welsh.*

What makes this all the more alarmingly funny is knowing that its author, only a few months afterward, would appear at Buckingham Palace to receive the Queen's Medal for Poetry. It is just as well that the heir to the throne seems not to have been present.

Typical, at any rate, of Stevie Smith's bedrock irreverence is a largely unfavorable essay on *Murder in the Cathedral* that was her contribution, "a very un-birthday present," to a symposium when T. S. Eliot turned seventy. A giggling "mouse-in-the-wainscot" subversiveness animated many of her friendships, as it did the one with George Stonier, an editor who may be said to have discovered her as a writer. The closest of these connections seem to have been with women; among the people Frances Spaulding has tracked down is an unnamed woman with whom Stevie had a brief affair. (The question of whether her friendship with George Orwell was ever anything more than that is discussed, but remains unsettled.) As a child she had been daring and gregarious; but like many gregarious people, at a deeper level she remained intensely solitary.

Without doubt the one person to whom Stevie Smith was

most deeply attached was Madge Spear, the "Lion Aunt" with whom she lived, in the same house, for over six decades. By comparison Marianne Moore, the looming presence of her mother notwithstanding, appears almost footloose. There may be a kind of wisdom here, comparable to that of Gerard Manley Hopkins in giving over his career to the Jesuits, since for a temperament so richly anarchic, some rock to lean on may be truly a matter of life and death.

But no such stability is without its cost. The house at One Avondale Road, in the London suburb of Palmers Green, was by all accounts a dreary one, with its overstuffed sitting room, its inconvenient kitchen, and the gloom of an enormous privet hedge outside. Stevie could, and repeatedly did, praise the Aunt who presided over her life there for being so solidly and completely ordinary. But her own nature, more even than most people's, was a bundle of mixed feelings and contrary impulses, and a part of it was implacably set against everything Madge Spear represented. "I don't care much for this meelyoo," Stevie declared in "Freddy," a famous early poem. "I don't anheimate mich in the la-la well-off suburban scene."

What she couldn't "anheimate" herself to was the "meelyoo" of the parish magazine, the social occasion at which, it is smotheringly reported, "A good time was had by all" (whence the title of her first book of poems). Not far off—waiting, as it were, in the wings—is the throttled loathing immortalized by John Osborne in *A Better Class of Person:* the letters signed, "Always in my thoughts, Mother," expressive of a routine so settled that the tiniest subverting of the expected comes as a betrayal. For sheer deadliness, this peculiarly English desolation far outstrips the looser, flashier bigotry that is its Stateside counterpart.

Madge Spear was not altogether a bigot—when her niece brought home an Indian radical, she listened, whether or not she believed all he told her of what had gone on under the British Raj—but as one whose favorite book concerned the suppression of a tribal uprising in Chitral, her jingoist tendencies may be imagined. As Stevie herself sadly observed, "It is mediocrity (though people cannot help being mediocre) that makes things so suffering for other people."

No wonder that so much of her mental energy went into subverting the expected. And no wonder that her manner was often bratty, even callous: in the very sharpness of her intelligence there remained something stunted and merely precocious, incapable of growing up. The bright upper register of her emotional range seems to have contained, as the nearest thing to joy, no more than an impudent glee. She would recognize this when she repudiated the "pseudo" and "brassy" tone of her first novel—and she did so again, more poignantly, when she wrote:

> I was much farther out than you thought
> And not waving but drowning.

Three months after writing what is now her most famous poem, Stevie Smith made an attempt at suicide. A sentence from a letter written years before—"there it is, death death death lovely death"—sounds strangely like an echo of Whitman. But that attempt on her own life, in July, 1953, places her instead in the company of Virginia Woolf, of Charlotte Mew, and most strikingly of Sylvia Plath, who had written Stevie a fan letter not long before her own self-inflicted death. One cannot but wonder what might have been had that attempt failed, and had she gone on living, and writing, as Stevie Smith did for very nearly another twenty years.

Her fascination with death, a friend once remarked, was the one thing that kept Stevie alive. But this is not quite true. Whatever the temptations of the morbid (she wrote a novel called *Married to Death,* which nobody wanted to publish), one element in her uneasy chemistry was severely classical. She could growl, "I am not God's little lamb / I am God's sick tiger." But somewhere in the lower, truer register of her emotional makeup was a sense of "the tears of things, and our mortality"—a line from the *Aeneid* she had learned as a schoolgirl, and which (as her biographer puts it) seems forever after to have "tolled in her mind." One feels, in considering what this book has to tell us, the bravery of a lifelong effort to contend, in one way or another, with the desolation of the ordinary.

In this she prefigures, above all, the late Philip Larkin. It is not only that he spent a large part of his life in Hull, where hers began. More tellingly, Philip Larkin was among the first to discern, beneath the overbrightness of what sounded like light verse, the submerged tolling he referred to as "the authority of sadness." Thus far her work has not received much more in the way of critical assessment. But perhaps one day Stevie Smith will be seen as having to some degree paved the way for a body of work whose upper register is distinguished by a spaciousness and clarity hers never achieved, but whose chief labor has been to unearth, in a dismaying time and likewise at great personal cost, something of value from the slagheap of ordinary life.

Seamus Heaney and the
Matter of Ireland

The claim laid on the imagination of readers in the two decades since *Death of a Naturalist* is now so powerful that a new book by Seamus Heaney inevitably means a lookout for familiar landmarks, signs, and affirmations of continuity. In *The Haw Lantern* (Farrar, Straus & Giroux, 1987), the continuity is present, but it is curbed by a newly gnomic severity. Perhaps the most extravagant single moment is one out of the irrecoverable past.

> Deep planted and long gone, my coeval
> Chestnut from a jam jar in a hole,
> Its heft and hush become a bright nowhere . . .

But the elegiac echo of Hopkins, an acknowledged early influence, as well as of Yeats, is typical only in its concern with something gone. Elsewhere in the memorial sequence of which it is a part, the language is blunter. A once companionable attachment to solid objects—the sandstone keepsake, "so reliably dense and bricky"; the iron spike from a defunct New Hampshire railway; the stone from Delphi—that figured in *Station Island,* has been superseded. This, from the opening sonnet of the sequence, is what we find in its place:

> A cobble thrown a hundred years ago
> Keeps coming at me, the first stone
> Aimed at a great-grandmother's turncoat brow.

Originally published in the *Boston Sunday Globe*, October 18, 1987.

This is continuity with a vengeance. We are plunged into the long-drawn-out sectarian conflict that the work of Seamus Heaney from the beginning has courteously asked us to bear with him: the Ireland of unhindered starvation, twice evoked in *Death of a Naturalist;* of resistance ("Requiem for the Croppies"); of repression ("Act of Union"); and of martial law that dominates the elegies in *Field Work* and that suffuses the title sequence of *Station Island.* It is the same theme that (in "Leaving") follows the poet to England,

> down from Ely's Lady Chapel,
> the sweet tenor latin
> forever banished,
> the sumptuous windows
> threshed clear by Thomas Cromwell—

that other, earlier Cromwell, before the Oliver whom Milton with high-minded bigotry celebrated for the invasion Yeats would later recall with outrage and horror.

The image of the self-righteously hurled first stone recurs, with an almost biblical emphasis, in another poem whose language is newly, and typically, bare and cryptic:

> Let it be like the judgment of Hermes,
> God of the stone heap, where the stones were verdicts
> Cast solidly at his feet, piling deep around him
> Until he stood waist deep in the cairn
> Of his apotheosis . . . .
>
> ("The Stone Verdict")

Other recurrences likewise show a change. In an early essay, Heaney recalls the pump at the back door of his childhood, from which five households drew water and which for him "centered and staked the imagination, made its foundation of the *omphalos* itself." That pump, that source, appears over and over in his poems. We find it now updated:

> Remember when our electric pump gave out,
> Priming it with bucketfuls, our idiotic rage

And hangdog phone-calls to the farm next door
For somebody please to come and fix it?
And when it began to hammer on again,
Jubilation at the tap's full force, the sheer
Given fact of water . . . .

                               ("Grotus and Coventina")

In the earlier "Gifts of Rain," dating to 1972,

A man wading lost fields
breaks the pane of flood

a flower of mudwater blooms up to his reflection . . . .

This is typical of the water imagery we associate with Heaney—
who wrote in that same early essay of "the invitation of watery
ground" as having "an immediate and deeply peaceful attrac-
tion." In a new poem, an elegy for a niece killed in an accident,
he speaks of how "everyone is loath / To trust the rain's
softsoaping ways." The central fact of water becomes, in "Hail-
stones," at once a missile and emblem of transience and instabil-
ity: "a small hard ball / of burning water running from my
hand."

    Drastic reductions and diminishments occur throughout
The Haw Lantern. The exuberance of mad Sweeney "praising
aloud all of the trees of Ireland" is gone along with the poet's
own coeval. Whatever the cause, he clearly acknowledges what
is happening. "Christ's sickle has been in the undergrowth," he
tells us in the poem that begins the book: "The script grows
hard and Merovingian." Where there was unpruned foliage
there is now calligraphy. Of course, there is a long tradition
behind this, a tradition older than Irish Christianity.

The letters of this alphabet were trees.
The capitals were orchards in full bloom,
The lines of script like briars coiled in ditches.

And Shakespeare's wooden *O,* the great globe itself, as seen by
the astronaut—

all he has sprung from,
The risen, aqueous, singular, lucent O
Like a magnified and buoyant ovum

has been condensed. The self-containing sphere, whose em-
blematic minuscule seems to be everywhere, is most vividly
embodied by the much-in-little of the title poem:

The wintry haw is burning out of season,
crab of the thorn, a small light for small people,
wanting no more from them but that they keep
the wick of self-respect from dying out,
not having to blind them with illumination.

The hawthorn, a hedge tree, is, of course, one of the land-
marks throughout Heaney territory. There are the "haw-lit
hedges" of the long poem "Kinship" in *North,* the "spit blood
of a last few haws and rose hips" in "The Loaning." Here,
grown urgent in its diminishment, the image of the small light
attaches itself to

the roaming shape of Diogenes
with his lantern seeking one just man;
so you end up scrutinized from behind the haw
he holds up at eye-level on its twig . . . .

"Tightness and nilness," the "cradled guns that hold you un-
dercover / and everything is pure interrogation"; "an old dis-
dain of sweet talk and excuses": The stance is, if not quite
desperate, almost desperately wary—wary of outcomes, of
rhetoric, of the very properties of language. For Heaney, the
guarded position is not exactly a departure. In an essay pub-
lished in 1972, he described the process of writing as "a kind
of somnambulist encounter between masculine will and intelli-
gence and feminine clusters of image and emotion," and went
on to say: "I suppose the feminine element for me involves
the matter of Ireland, and the masculine strain is drawn from
the involvement with English literature. . . . I teach English
literature, publish in London, but the English tradition is not
ultimately home. . . . Grove and park," he continued, writing

of the great houses from which the plantation—so called—of
Ireland was accomplished, "—they do not reach me as a fibre
from a tap-root but remind me of the intricate and various
foliage of history and culture that I grew up beneath. . . . If
you like, I began as a poet when my roots were crossed with
my reading."

In "Station Island," the ghost of James Joyce is heard to
declare,

> ". . . The English language
> belongs to us . . .
> That subject people stuff is a cod's game,
> infantile, like your peasant pilgrimage. . . ."

It seems clear from these new poems, however, that Heaney's
own distrust, not simply of English, but of language itself, is
unallayed. The way the Irish have with our language must
derive in part from their peculiar relation to it. Oscar Wilde's
one unflawed masterpiece is a dazzling subversion, anatomiz-
ing his own distrust of everything people say. The tran-
scendant posturings of Yeats were a loftier strategy for deal-
ing with a like situation. The diffident Synge gave attentive
ear to the sound of Gaelic, and got little comfort for the care
he took. Continued subornings and depredations—the rot-
ting of diction that Emerson took note of a century and a half
ago—are sufficient to make all forms of communication sus-
pect. Hints of something like this run through *The Haw Lan-
tern*. Titles such as "From the Frontier of Writing" and "From
the Land of the Unspoken" suggest what would hitherto have
seemed unlikely—that Heaney territory in fact adjoins that of
the towering Samuel Beckett. Heaney himself is by now a very
famous man. For all his apparently easygoing public manner,
in a time when so little that is said is fit to be trusted, this new
book confirms him as one who is, to use a word he favors,
reliable—a poet of the very strictest integrity.

James Merrill and
the Winter Maisie Died

In "Keats and Cats" (*Essays and Studies*, 1962) Robert Gittings brought together all the references to cats in the poems of Keats. The most considerable of these is a Miltonic parody that opens: "Cat! who hast past thy Grand Climacteric," and concludes:

> . . . for all
> The tail's tip is nicked off—and though the fists
> Of many a Maid have given thee many a maul,
> Still is that fur as soft as when the lists
> In youth thou enter'dst on glass bottled wall.

Alike in age and experience, as well as gender, is the

> Caller the color of good smoke blown through the years
> Into this dumb scarred mug he lifts to say:
> "Huh! Not want *me!* Man, the whole world wants *cats!*"

in "Clearing the Title"—scrappily upholding Gittings's own notion of cats as the chief amenity of a settled household.

So much for what might have seemed a promising correspondence. The fact is that the poems of James Merrill are more often concerned with the canine than with the feline kind. It must be NO ACCIDENT that one of the most famous Merrill poems, notorious for its punning final line, concerns

---

Originally published in *Verse*, July, 1988. Reprinted by permission.

"red, satyr-thighed / Michael, the Irish setter," companion of the child roaming the corridors of the broken home. The much later "Lost in Translation" speaks of a "collie who did everything but talk." Oh yes, there is also something about a tiger skin and a "minor lion attending on Gerome"; but it is "the dog's tail thumping" that comes alive. From his earliest years, this is a poet whose inclination is toward the dog, literally the small boy's best friend. The adult poet, in "After Greece," would raise a question:

> . . . The next week . . . I sailed for home.
> But where is home—these walls?
> These limbs? The very spaniel underfoot
> Races in sleep, toward what?

In the absence of such canine associations—it could be argued—*Mirabell's Book of Numbers* might have stopped dead before it got under way. In Athens after a session at the Ouija board, the doorbell rings; JM excuses himself to discover that

> . . . no one's there. Or only an unfamiliar
> Black dog, leg lifted at our iron gate,
> Marking his territory.

Months later, in Stonington, the board spells out

> . . . WE ARE THE SONS OF CAIN
>
> David looks up in genuine alarm:
> But these are devils, they're the fallen angels!
> JM: I wonder. Wouldn't a surefire devil
> Pretend to be someone nicer? And why should They
> Speak of leading us back to Paradise?
> DJ: Why shouldn't they? They want it back.
> They're fighting us, like Faust, to get it back.
> JM: Well then, we now know what our black
> Dog in Athens meant. There's one in *Faust;*
> A kind of feeler Mephistopheles
> Sends out before appearing. A black poodle.
> DJ: Let's stop *right now.*

Four books later, DJ still admits to fright, JM is sanguine:

> If there's no accident, all things alive
> Or dead that touch us—Ephraim, the black dog
> In Athens . . .
> Are droplets in a "probability fog"
> With us as nucleus.

Toward the end of Book 9, the worst scare yet occurs:

> En route, the same sun-flooded evening,
> To dine back country, something black gives chase
> High-spiritedly barking—ah, slow down!
> As in a bad dream the dog veers, is hit,
> Not hard but . . . D and I walk back to it
> Struggling, hind legs motionless.

What then of the transcribed words of Mirabell, the fallen angel: I WILL BE THE WOUNDED BLACK HOUND OF HEAVEN AT YR DOOR ? Later, the two of them surmise that

> The black dog, good as new, had known DJ,
> Bounded in perfect rapture to the car
> No accident: Or else a dog that died
> So many deaths each day,
> Emotional or cellular,
> That death no longer . . . .

Which is all we hear of him henceforth, unless one counts a passage in *Scripts for the Pageant* comparing Gabriel, the Shy Brother among the Archangels, to

> THE SOUNDING BASS
> IN THE QUARTET   OR PITCH INAUDIBLE
> EXCEPT TO A BLACK DOG . . . .

Cats as occult familiars, on the other hand, make their appearance early. In the Dramatis Personae near the beginning of *The Book of Ephraim*, Maya Deren's Village flat is described:

```
                    . . . underfoot
         The latest in a lineage of big, black
         Strangely accident-prone Haitian cats.
```

That is one level. At another, the (rehabilitated) fallen angel Mirabell declares: "BUT THE GREAT / MIRACLE IS THE REINCARNATION OF THE GODS." Akhnaton and Nefertiti, he goes on to say, "RESENTFUL LIKE ALL CHILDREN OF HAVING TO OBEY SUPERIOR GOD FIGURES," accordingly banished the cat from the Egyptian pantheon, along with the snake and the falcon, in favor of the sun-disk.

I think there might be some connection here with a poem in *The Fire Screen* (1969) in which a lizard, a kitten, and a scarab beetle are seen as envoys of "the brittle pharaohs in the vale of Hence." The subject is fear:

```
         The total experience depending, as it does
         Upon modulation into a brighter key
         Of terror we survive to play . . . .
```

Going still deeper into the human past, Mirabell declares:

```
         DOUBT IS YR HELL JM & YOURS
         DJ IS FEAR. HELL IS THE CAVE OF PSYCHE & HARKS
            BACK
         TO ONE MORNING WHEN APECHILD'S PATH FROM
            HIS IST WATERHOLE
         IN EDEN CROSSD THAT OF A FIERCE CROUCHING
            CAT . . . .
```

NO ACCIDENT, then, that a work whose central theme and premise is reincarnation should consider the proverbial nine lives:

```
      Instinctive pupils glowered in the tomb.
      THE CAT LOOK IS A LOCK WHERE CONSCIOUSNESS
      RISES each nine lives an inch?
```

Or, in "Words for Maria," "Curiosity long since killed the cat / inside you." Concerning Maya Deren we learn, in *The Book of Ephraim*, that while she was still alive, during a session at the Ouija board the summer Wallace Stevens died, she had been told she was in her "FIRST LAST ONLY LIFE . . . The cat she felt kept dying in her stead / Did exactly that. She was *its* patron." A moment later,

> Maya stiffens. She has heard
> A faint miaow—we all have. In comes Maisie,
> Calico self-possession six weeks old,
> Already promising to outpoise by ounces
> Ephraim as the household heavyweight.

That would have been in 1956. Later, we're told,

> Delinquency was rising. Maisie made
> Eyes at shadows—time we had her spayed.

This was, alas, done. *Water Street* (1962) contains an extended tribute:

> When you came home without your sex
> You hid in the cupboard under the sink.
> Its gasps and gurglings must have helped somehow.
>
> The second noon you ventured forth,
> A silent star, furred up to tragic eyes,
> Hazarding recognition in a restaurant.
>
> . . . .
> (If eyes could shriek, and if they were ever
> Eyes, those chalcedony bonfires): *O*
> *Scarpia! Avanti à Dio!*

NO ACCIDENT, surely, that *The Book of Ephraim* has JM say, "Like Tosca hadn't we / Lived for art and love?"—or that Maisie, and not Michael the red setter ("The Victor Dog" is not about a dog but about art), is awarded the notice of an entire poem. Or that, for this reader at any rate, one of the most poignantly felt passages in the whole of *The Changing Light at Sandover* is the following:

Greece was too much for Maisie. She'd grown old
Flights above the street. Now, worse than vile
Food, vile customs, than finding her place in my bed—
In *her* bed—taken, came these myriad
Voices [Devil-baby altos, gibbous moans]
Undulating over clammy tile
Toward the half mad old virgin Henry James
Might have made of her, and this James had.

The side of me that deeply took her side
Was now a wall. Turning her face to it
She read the blankness there, and died—

What has happened need not be surmised, since we are given
to know: it is the advent of Strato, whose "qualities / All are
virtues back in '64 . . . Shine of light green eyes, enthusiasm /
Panting and warm across the kindly chasm." But as Ephraim
spells it out on the Ouija board: MY DEAR HE'S IN / HIS
IST MANS LIFE . . . THE UNSEASONED SOUL / LIKE
QUICKLY BURNING TIMBER WARMS A BED / TOO
SOON OF ASHES. . . .

It was this same Strato, presumably, who threaded a harness
about the scarab beetle, and around whose head "whirred a
living emerald satellite": it might almost have been one of
those chalcedony bonfires, heedlessly plucked from its socket.
Such is the charm, such the inseparability of that charm from
danger:

Phaedra, extracted from your jacket lining,
Flung herself like a bird against the glass—
who that same night lay on your heart and purred—

as Maisie had slept once with her full weight on the speaker's
heart, "your motors and my breathing reconciled." Whether
this Phaedra or some other is the feline of "Flying from
Byzantium"—

Our linen's at the laundromat.
What will become of the gray cat
I'd rather not conjecture.

As for my regular lecture
—Kindness to Animals—I'll spare you that—

I too find it preferable not to conjecture.
To be quite accurate, it must be noted that in the related
"Last Words"

It's noon, it's dawn, it's night,
I am the dog that dies
In the deep street of Troy
Tomorrow, long ago—

as it would be inaccurate to ignore that a villainous white cat
named Grimes is responsible for the extraordinary nastiness
of "The Summer People." Nevertheless, Part O of *The Book of
Ephraim* is climactic in more ways than one. "With Maisie
gone, and Maya gone," JM and DJ are "that much less
equipped to face the Sphinx."

. . . The mere word "animal" a skin
Through which its old sense glimmers, *of the soul.*

—But oh the cold! Bare pillow next to mine. . . .
While, outside, cats and dogs just keep on raining.

Rereading Howard Moss

Howard Moss kept two appointment books, one at home and one at his office, and as a result he often committed himself to be in two places at once. That was what happened when my first meeting with him, in the fall of 1979, had to be rescheduled. By then he was a very important person in my life, not simply the magazine editor to whom I now regularly sent things but also the first such to accept a poem of mine, aside from a teenage indiscretion that appeared in a college magazine. Arriving elated but anxious in the lobby of the Algonquin, I had no trouble recognizing him—which is more than the headwaiter did. Unable to get the latter's attention, this major power in the small world of poets shrugged and murmured, "We'll just go down the street." It was, I couldn't help telling myself, at least partly my fault for not looking like somebody famous. The fact remains that Howard didn't either. He could have been, and was, somebody's uncle: a niece and two nephews were his immediate survivors.

That incident was typical of the Howard Moss I knew, and it endeared him to me forever. His two appointment books, down to the final week of his life, were crowded with names—dozens, scores, hundreds perhaps, of people who loved, revered, and worried over him as I did. I could never think of him as gregarious, but clearly he went out a lot. Now and then I would see him at some gathering. About once a year he would come for dinner and what we referred to as a Mozart evening. From his own "Incomplete and Disputed Sonatas"—

Originally published in *Parnassus* 15, no. 1 (1989). Reprinted by permission.

> The G-Minor Quintet saying
> How nothing lasts
> But music by Mozart—

there could be no doubt of his views on that hallowed subject. Though I don't recall that we ever played the Glyndebourne recording of *Così fan tutte* from beginning to end, that was a fixed point of reference. Sound and movement, the sung or the spoken word were central to the way he lived. The news of Suzanne Farrell's return to the ballet stage struck me first of all with a pang of grief that Howard was not here to see it. And the one thing I ever heard him say of his own craft as a poet was, as nearly as I can recall, "It ought to be clear to anybody that all I do is put in the left hand."

And so, I suppose, it ought to have been to anyone taking note of titles, from the very early "Clichés for Piano and Orchestra" down through "Piano Practice." Going on to look at the texts, you find "the song recital / The rain was trying to compose this morning" in "Bay Days"; or "A moment so made up of other moments / No one can tell one famous variation / From another" in "The Restaurant Window." There are many others. And so when, in "A Lesson from Van Gogh," the painter says, "Take my ear," we can be sure we are on to something. The injunction is to reach and captivate in the manner of Perdita's daffodils taking the winds of March with beauty. The lines

> Speechless tree and animal and bird
> Vein dreams with meaning, often blurred—

express in rhyme what would later turn up as prose assertion: "Poetry is essentially the use of words to express the nonverbal." That it should aspire to the condition of music is endorsed, but with a caveat: not to a condition that goes floating off into some vague empyrean of melody.

> "Talk to me,"
> Van Gogh was saying, "I am not a tree,
> A fish, a serpent, lion, pig, or jay."

That last plea—"Talk to me," not "Sing to me," not croon, or intone, or whatever, but *talk*—is no happenstance. The clearest early influence on Howard Moss's poetry—as for so many of his contemporaries—is that of W. H. Auden, whom he would later describe as having

> restored to poetry what it had for a long time lacked, a relevant human voice. After the Victorian and the Edwardian poets had had their say, the problem was somehow to construct a style out of the real that was neither banal nor elevated. It became the great task of this century's poetry, a labor that often produced the humdrum at one end of the scale and the rhetorical at the other.

If there is little, as the century ends, to encourage a belief that the task is near completion, the state of affairs is not one to blame Howard for. After Auden, the poet he came most to admire, the one who seems to have had a predominant effect on his own poetry is Elizabeth Bishop. The reason is clear from his praising her as "one of the true masters of tone," as having "an absolute sense of what the English language can do, of how much to say, how much to leave unsaid."

In a poet who has even a painter saying, "Take my ear," such concern with tone is no surprise.* That rhetoric should have come to be suspect is understandable. For Howard Moss himself, however, it becomes "a dirty word only when it is used to mask or ignore the truth." And he went on to assert: "The fear of rhetoric makes most modern writing dull. Reality is reduced to a kind of recipe book of facts in which categorical description becomes a substitute for perception." Concerning the poetic voice in particular, he shrewdly observed:

---

*What is surprising—or anyhow I find it so, at a time when poets go traveling about reading their works aloud as never before in history—is the continued prevalence of a certain mannered, self-conscious, even portentous delivery, among poets commonly regarded as having eschewed the artifices of rhetoric. Where does it come from? Pound, maybe? No one I have asked seems to have a clear answer.

The insistence on not being formal, or stuck-up, or mannered, the freedom to use any kind of language, the emphasis on being real and spontaneous are all to the good, but they are also symptoms. People who are natural do not ask themselves how to be natural. Art is not nature.

What made him admire Elizabeth Bishop, at any rate, is the seemingly effortless way in which her poetry brought art and nature together, so as after all to be one and the same:

> observation and temperament have become inseparable; telling the truth is a form of human sympathy, not a moral imperative or scientific curiosity. . . . A clearly lighted equanimity allows for every note of the scale. . . . In being herself and telling the truth, she supersedes manners by setting superior standards.

Out of simple prudence, Howard Moss made few statements in print concerning living poets. Elizabeth Bishop, then alive but in Brazil, was a notable exception; James Schuyler is another whose reclusiveness seemed to allow for an extended notice. More often than with poets, living or not, his critical writings dealt with the masters of prose. Foremost among these are two not often linked—Proust and Chekhov. Midway in his critical study, *The Magic Lantern of Marcel Proust,* Howard speaks of the "bedazzlements that outweigh . . . lucidity." On the final page, however, he observes that Proust, "because he was so greatly enchanted, is the greatest of disenchanters"—a title for which Anton Chekhov might seem to be the contender par excellence. Howard admired them both as truth-tellers, but also as artists whose works embody something analogous to music. "Proust, the most tonal of all fiction writers," he wrote, "is also one of the most accurate"; and elsewhere:

> He dissected snobbery, down to the ultimate fishbone . . . . His portrait of the cravenness, vulgarity, and pettiness, the inner corruption of people who held power in their hands is icily cold and crystal clear.

As for Chekhov: "It is hard to think of another writer whose work is at once so objective and so personal. . . . His force as an artist derives from his being meticulously invisible and miraculously audible." He goes on to say: "More than most authors, Chekhov gives the impression of not being one, of simply observing life and writing it down." And:

It is tone alone that turns Chekhov's stories into poems, his plays into music, even in translation. Tone is the most important quality of good writing and the hardest to define. . . . It is what is meant, perhaps, by the phrase "between the lines." Something that is there but which cannot be pointed to specifically.

Defining Chekhov's "absolute control of tone," he discovers "a subtle and unique blend of melancholy, the farcical, and the ironic." This may be an answer to the question of whether *The Cherry Orchard* is or is not a comedy. And in any event it is as apt a characterization as we are likely to find of Howard Moss.

No one I ever knew was more genuinely and habitually kind than he was—as though he had consciously adopted Chekhov's maxim: "One must not humiliate people—that is the chief thing." If this is so, Howard's poem "Fern Dying" hilariously indicates the effort thereby entailed:

"Here are my versions of some René Char
Poems . . . *Be frank! Tell* me—are they *good?*
Or *bad,* as the case may be! Don't spare
The rod! And here's my essay on Cocteau
(We were too *close* for him to mention me . . .)—
It's *still* unpublished! Tell me . . . *really! Why?*"
. . . .
I sound like Madame Blank. I mean between
The lines . . . Or in them. That old pathetic bore!
That dying generation with no song!
And with that, unexpected tears. Poor lady!
Poor fern! The room is gravid with self-pity.
My ballpoint pen is writing something:
                                              "Dear
Madame Blank,
                        Wednesday will be fine."

A benevolence just tinged with sadness was what I saw as Howard's habitual expression. But now and then it would go prim—a signal that he was about to deliver himself of something outrageous. His poems are full of such things. Often the thing is a pun, as when he exhorts the dying fern,

> Bloom! Bloom! Like Molly in *Ulysses*. Joyce.
> A spore is not a flower. Jean Cocteau?

The word-play was often, though not necessarily, literary, and tended to ramify. "The Love Songs of Horatio Alger, Jr." are a homage to their predecessor, with a central spasm of terror ("I see the madman's eyes insist / On taking children home to bed"), and after that a jolt toward a familiar subject:

> These dollar signs that are my eyes,
> This ticker tape that is my brain . . . .

It is remarkable, and no accident, how often the poems refer, with a gesture of sardonic resignation, to the omnipresence of money. It is the explicit subject of one of his two plays, a farce called *The Folding Green* that opens out into one teasing, interminable pun: besides the eponymous currency, the title refers successively to an evening dress, a holder of debentures, a shutter, the painter's craft ("I fold in some green"), and finally everything in sight. "I hear this play is folding," the final spoken line, is followed by a direction: "The lighting on the stage turns green"—the purpose of the enterprise having been set forth as "a last stand for the lost art of the epigram." There is a dedication to Jean Stafford, and it is easy to imagine the two of them going at it together, trading such one-liners as "Foundations consist of untalented people revenging themselves on the talented," or "Do you know anything about money? . . . It's what people exchange between emotions."

Recurrent allusions to this latter subject are no joke:

> We'd like to be where money talks,
> For all the rest is gibberish . . .

followed by

> At Cold Cash, where the castle is,
> Or where it is supposed to be,
> Nobody ever dies, it seems;
> They just go on—from first to last
> A series of monotonies—

Altogether, what Howard saw as the truth about us, about human behavior, turns out grimmer and more despairing than I wanted to suppose.

> Think
> Of houses, dinners, all mendacious calm,
> Then, rising at the edge of Paradise, a slum
>
> In whose bleak tenements some poor souls sit
> Forever, staring into a machine . . .

He is preeminently a poet of the city—indeed, it is now clear to me that he is the preeminent poet of New York City and its extensions eastward: not only Manhattan and the Hamptons, exuberantly celebrated in "Stars"; but also and no less, in "Long Island Springs," the little houses with back gardens, of

> . . . those lifelong two
> Transplanted figures in a suburb who
> Loved me without saying, "I love you"—

and the cemetery in Queens where

> The black funeral parlor limousines
> Just make it up the narrow aisles. . . .

He is also the poet of Village roof gardens and water trucks, and the peculiar metropolitan solitudes evoked by a single perfect line, "I see the building you are working in," or by, in "Winter Botany,"

> . . . this city of four million love affairs
> That has its night life on. . . .

What has tended to go unnoticed, given the deprecatory primness with which he serves up the ironies of disappointment, is the moral historian behind it:

> ... two fixed ideas
> Whose narrow apertures of sky in time
> Will house the slums of 1989. . . .

Or, at Miami Beach:

> Was Nature a snob,
> Distributing shorefronts only to the rich?
> The poor have come to the right conclusion.

Or, once again from the relentless, complex, and allusive "Buried City," which is perhaps his masterpiece:

> Graffiti on the walls read *mene, mene,*
> *Tekel, upharsin,*—and the city fell.

In all this, as in so much, Howard Moss could be Chekhov writing to Tikhonov: "I only wished to tell people honestly: look at yourselves; see how badly and boringly you live." He saw clearly what mattered, and set it down: "Marcel's grandmother is the moral centre of his social vision . . . the single human person in Proust's novel who is capable of feeling human love." The same values are affirmed in "The Gift to Be Simple," an early work—and lest there be any question, are reaffirmed in "Einstein's Bathrobe," a jeu d'esprit that would have occurred to nobody but Howard, and which he deliberately placed at the end of his last collection:

> At tea at Mercer Street every afternoon
> His manners went beyond civility,
> Kindness not having anything to learn. . . .

If, as is undoubtedly true, Howard Moss has been undervalued as a poet, that is partly the fault of those who knew him. He and his work are of a piece; the tone of the poems is the tone of the living person. Reading and rereading them now, however, I not only find them funny in precisely the way Howard was funny, but also, both between and in the lines, finer, larger, more luminously charged than his endearingly temperate demeanor had led me to suppose.

The last time Howard came to dinner, there was some quiet talk—but with no premonition, otherwise the subject would not have come up at all—of the dread and fear of hospitals. It was the last time I saw him. The last time I spoke with him, he was in New York Hospital, too frightened and depressed to talk for more than a minute or two. At the time he died I happened to be in Houston, where he had many friends. Our awed disbelief gave way to thinking how greatly he would be missed, and then to which of his poems we liked best. I did not know then quite how much we had lost, or the true extent of what remains.

Robert Frost and the
Better Half of Poetry

Some years ago I came upon one of those single passages that
can be so arresting as to call for an immediate rearrangement
of one's ideas. The context was a *Georgia Review* essay by Jona-
than Holden (later reprinted in *The Rhetoric of the Contemporary
Lyric,* Indiana University Press, 1980):

> by and large the emphasis on metaphor . . . in American po-
> etry of the 1970s is a natural outgrowth of the recession of
> music in favor of closure as the dominant convention that
> seems at times virtually to define "poetry."

The recession of music in favor of closure: that was the phrase
that leaped at me from the page, and made me wonder all at
once where I was, where I had been, and what was going to
happen next. At the time I had not so much as heard of
Barbara Herrnstein Smith's *Poetic Closure: A Study of How Po-
ems End* (Chicago, 1968). If I had, no doubt I would have
taken note of her statement that "analogues between music
and poetry are always suggestive, particularly so in connection
with closure," and of her reference to the "conventionalized"
situation in, for example, Petrarchan love poetry; as well as, a
little further on, her observation that "the concluding lines of
many sixteenth-century poems . . . would be as alien to a mod-
ern poem as a pavan in a modern dance." If what Jonathan

Adapted from a paper read at The Frost Place, Franconia, New
Hampshire, and first published as "The Better Half of Poetry" in
Grand Street (Summer 1985). Reprinted by permission.

Holden proposed is correct, the conventions of lyric poetry have so far departed from those of the sixteenth century as to have produced "the poem that is all metaphor and that is *without* music" (my italics). He was writing of things in the seventies. Now that not only the seventies have come to an end, but the eighties as well, what new thing sits waiting to leap off the page? For this reader, one such thing is a concept encountered for the first time in an essay on A. R. Ammons, in Willard Spiegelman's *The Didactic Muse* (Princeton, 1990):

> Current literary wisdom holds that all literature gives prominence to the *lisible*, because language is inscriptive. No priority is granted to voice, transcendent reality, or "world" because language itself creates, commands, and precedes the meanings that it inscribes, submerging its "referents" more and more deeply into a scribal palimpsest. I do not wish to tackle, let alone refute, Derridean orthodoxies. . . . Still, it seems legitimate to credit Ammons with having created a poetry, like that of William Carlos Williams, that is genuinely unhearable.

The prominence of the lisible, as opposed to the merely audible: if this is indeed the way things are going, one can only conclude that the recession from music continues—toward what end I myself quail at the very thought of. It's not that aural poetry is dead: pop music on the airwaves and rap all over the place prove otherwise, not to mention the food-hawkers who are still at it, half a century after Gershwin put the strawberry woman and the deviled-crab man of Charleston onto the operatic stage—or, indeed, the caller at Penn Station whose chanted Allll-a-bo-*oht!* surely qualifies as an aria. None of this is exactly literature, at any rate literature as Mary Renault in *The Praise Singer* conceived of Simonides conceiving it at the beginning of the fifth century B.C.:

> So what can I do, unless I'm to be remembered only by what's carved in marble? *Tell them in Lakedaimon, passerby, that here, obedient to their word, we lie.* They'll remember *that*. . . . Men forget how to write upon the mind. To hear, and to keep: that is our heritage from the Sons of Homer. Sometimes I think I

shall die their only heir. . . . I shall leave my scrolls, like the potter's cup and the sculptor's marble, for what they're worth. Marble can break; the cup is a crock thrown in the well; paper burns warm on a winter night. I have seen too much pass away. . . . The true songs are still in the minds of men.

What happens when the true songs are no longer in the minds of men? We are seeing what happens. Memory is elsewhere—on library shelves, squirreled into microfilm, cramming the reductive labyrinth of a microchip. The only exceptions to its seemingly irreversible atrophy are among the illiterate. We are drowning in print, and yet (with a few rare and glorious exceptions) nobody remembers anything. In my darker moments I wonder sometimes whether anybody *reads* anything, aside from those who do so because they earn their keep that way—the literary theoreticians and (can it truly be?) those whose function is now to give them employment. In moments less glum, I still wonder whether, so far as the printed page is concerned, the aural, the hearable, the ear itself, are on their way to being regarded as passé. From a review of my own work I learned that it owed "everything to the eye and rather less to the ear." Well, that shook me. For as long as I can remember, however interesting the look of things (my earliest ambition having been to be a painter), in poetry the sound came first. The better half of poetry, Robert Frost called it.

> The ear [he wrote] is the only true writer and the only true reader. I have known people who could read without hearing the sentence sounds and they were the fastest readers. Eye readers we call them. They can get the meaning by glances. But they are bad readers because they miss the best part of what a good writer puts into his work.

He was referring to the kind of blank-verse dialogue you find all through *North of Boston*—blank verse like this, from "A Hundred Collars":

> I like to find folks getting out in spring,
> Raking a dooryard, working near the house.
> Later they get out further in the fields.

> Everything's shut sometimes except the barn;
> The family's all away in some back meadow.

That's a Yankee voice, and what makes it lively has been neatly spelled out by Frost himself:

> I am never more pleased than when I can get the very regular preestablished accent of blank verse, and the irregular accent and measure of speaking intonation, into strained relation. I like to drag and break the intonation across the metre as waves first comb and then break stumbling along the shingle.

He also knew how to slow down the pace, for an effect that is not a bit colloquial—as in this monologue by a census-taker who comes upon a house with nobody in it:

> This house in one year fallen into decay
> Filled me with no less sorrow than the houses
> Where Asia wedges Africa from Europe.
> Nothing was left to do that I could see. . . .

That deprecatory drop is pure Frost, and he fell into it often—letting you know that though some rather grand ruminations occasionally slip past, he's still the same pawky rural character. Nobody was ever going to catch him opening all the stops, the way Spenser had:

> The trembling ghosts with sad amazed mood,
> Chattring their yron teeth, and staring wide
> With stony eyes, and all the hellish brood
> Of feends infernall flockt on every side,
> To gaze on earthly wight that with the Night durst ride.

You're not going to catch him being grandly polemical either, the way Milton was:

> Avenge O Lord Thy slaughtered saints, whose bones
> Lie scattered on the Alpine mountains cold. . . .

Nobody writes like that these days, and it's not hard to imagine why. Humankind has simply been put in its place too unmistakably, has been taken in by its own overweenings, and then shown up for a dolt, a few times too often to leave room for all-out sublimity any more. Just why this should make poets wary of open vowel sounds ("Ay me! whilst thee the shores, and sounding Seas / Wash far away, where ere thy bones are hurled"), I'm not so sure, but it must be the same reason opera is so often thought of as not grand but ridiculous—and how we all do fear and dread to be that! What interests me about Frost, though, is how in his own way, with his own resolutely middling intentions, he does arrive at a kind of grandeur. He was not going to think of writing another "Lycidas." All the same, in "Once by the Pacific," he used simple couplets and still did justice to an ancient theme:

> It looked as though a night of dark intent
> Was coming, and not only a night, an age.
> Someone had better be prepared for rage.
> There would be more than ocean-water broken
> Before God's last *Put out the light* was spoken.

Milton's grand open O is made into a smaller sound: broken, spoken in those falling final syllables—a sort of cutting of sublimity down to size. But it's there all the same: the echo is there in the language for us to hear, when it's given a chance to be heard.

Nobody would accuse Robert Frost of being lush, either—in fact, as Howard Moss memorably put it, his Yankee wariness showed itself by refusing to be either naked or gorgeous. But there are poems of his that, though chilly by comparison with, say, "The murmurous haunt of flies on summer eves," do contain an almost Keatsian synesthesia:

> Let them think twice before they use their powers
> To blot out and drink up and sweep away
> These flowery waters and these watery flowers

in "Spring Pools," or

And with these sky-flakes down in flurry on flurry
There is more unmixed color on the wing
Than flowers will show for days unless they hurry

in "Blue-Butterfly Day"; or, in a poem more famous for the
sense, the almost sixteenth-century closure of its "what to
make of a diminished thing," than for the internal melody of

He says the early petal-fall is past
When pear and cherry bloom went down in showers
On sunny days a moment overcast;
And comes the other fall we name the fall.
He says the highway dust is over all.

I'm not trying to separate the melody from the meaning of
"The Oven Bird"—only to say that the melody is there: the
sound of the English language being turned into music.

It was a dryer, sparer sound, by the time Frost took it up;
and when you consider Wallace Stevens, it would seem that
the drying-up process had gone a bit further:

The lacquered loges huddled there
Mumbled zay-zay and a-zay, a-zay.

But even that jazzy little buzz would seem to be on its way out.
Consider, for a last example, the unmistakable tone (lisible or
whatever) of A. R. Ammons:

probably this is why nature says nothing—
it has nothing to say

is an extreme example—as is

we were talking about our MFA program
(pogrom) in Creative Writing when I said
should we, can we, professionalize
delight

Irresistible though I find this, the music is a vibration in the
brain rather than the ear. Can it be that what's in store for us is
indeed the poverty of living elsewhere than in a physical

world?* People, including poets, living more and more inside their own heads: is this what's happening? Is it why people turn out in such droves for poetry readings, the merely lisible and inscriptive notwithstanding? In a time when there is so little agreement about what the conventions are—if there even are any—anything is possible.

---

*Perhaps some sort of analogy may be drawn from the remarks of Arthur G. Danto in the *Nation* for July 9, 1990: "The history of Modernism is an erratic progress of self-purification. Thus the figure was discarded as contingent in pictorial representation by Abstractionists. Pictorial or illusionistic space was discarded as being inappropriate to abstraction, even if not filled with recognizable scenes and figures. Geometrical forms were discovered to be not altogether mandated by abstraction, which could be achieved by swipes of pigment across a flat surface. The brush stroke was demonstrably unrequired, as the drip-stick showed." And so on.

Made Things, Burrowings and Borrowings: Anthony Hecht

No less potent than the memory of things past that Proust sought to recapture, and that Lawrence wept like a child for, is their unwelcome, burrowing twin, the memory of what one would rather forget. This is the theme of "A Hill," with which *The Hard Hours* opens: the irruption of a childhood experience, not of safety (however illusory) but of desolation. The only detectable trace of life there is "a piece of ribbon snagged on a hedge"—the sort of detail, at once soiled and wistful, that is almost a badge of the poetry of Anthony Hecht—and the only sound

> What seemed the crack of a rifle. A hunter, I guessed;
> At least I was not alone. But just after that
> Came the soft and papery crash
> Of a great branch somewhere unseen falling to earth.
>
> And that was all, except for the cold and silence
> That promised to last forever.

One can't, or anyhow I can't, help connecting this with the conclusion of "The Most of It," Robert Frost's account of desolation in the wilderness. Is this a conscious and deliberate revision, in the way that, in "Rites and Ceremonies," the section subtitled "The Fire Sermon" is a revision of *The Waste Land*? I can't be sure, and I'm not sure that it matters. To pursue the comparison, in any event, is to observe how diametrically this most urbane of poets is unlike his rural predecessor. Even when, as in "Still Life," the poem is a departure from the urban scene, to where "nature is magnificently dumb," the very title is a sign of where the poet's concerns continue to reside. For him, the realm of everything that's made won't be annihilated, won't leave him alone. And so the calm of a lakeside before dawn is, he tells us, a "Tennysonian" one; the dew hanging from that quintessential made thing, a cobweb, is reminiscent of Steuben glass; the stillness throughout the universe is as of "ancient Chinese bowls." All of which might come off as overrefined, were it not for the made thing at the conclusion of the poem. Again, an undermining recollection is at work; the imaginary rifle of "A Hill" is now an actual, "cold, wet Garand" in the speaker's hands, "just before dawn, somewhere in Germany." This time the metaphysical chill finds its locus in history, a sense "of purposes and preordained events."

More forceful still is a rendering of the same theme in "Behold the Lilies of the Field," where details of the flaying of the Emperor Valerian ("And with him passed away the honor of Rome") emerge from what purports to begin as a psychoanalytic session. Grimmest of all, though muted in the telling, are the histories reenvisioned in "Rites and Ceremonies" by way of such artifacts as the roomful of human hair at Buchenwald, or the scaffold erected for the burning of Jews in medieval Strasbourg. In a world of made things, of such dazzlements and beguilings and such atrocities, what is the poet to do or say, whom the atrocities will not leave alone? About all I feel equipped to say concerning this powerful sequence is that with each rereading I find it more moving, and my admiration for it grows.

But I would also like to say something of a debt I am conscious of owing. It is my good fortune to have read "The Venetian Vespers" for the first time just as I was puzzling over how to begin a new poem. It concerned the experience of listening to the Beethoven piano sonata, Opus 111, with a renewed sense of the gulf between such supreme artifice and the ordinary existence of all who listen and admire and go back home to the multifarious aches and loathings, small or great, that the human sensibility is heir to. I can't say exactly how it happened, but the excitement I felt as I read "The

Venetian Vespers," and the example set by the accuracy that blenched at no detail, however minor or disagreeable—the wrinkled membrane on the surface of hot milk, the bubbles along the decaying stems of flowers in a vase—turned a key somewhere; and for the first time a subject that had hitherto seemed to me too grotesquely painful offered itself as the material of a poem, the very poem that had been set in motion by the Beethoven sonata—namely, a frightful exposure to poison ivy my father had once endured. But then the inspiration of the model poem became so potent that my own effort had to be put aside: something told me that the model's seamless pentameter couldn't be right for Beethoven, for the sonata with its violent extremes, its shifts and alternations, and it was months before my ear could emerge from its influence. The tribute of at least one smuggled-in item remains. Though there are instances when what looks like smuggling could be, and in fact is, sheer coincidence (as I know from red-faced experience; will John Ashbery believe, if it is brought to his notice, that I came upon his description of the stars as "myopic" only *after* using it in a poem of my own?), I can't but suppose that for the Piranesian catacombs that got into "Beethoven, Opus 111," the proximate source is the Piranesian *Carceri* of "The Venetian Vespers."

And there is more. Somewhat more recently, having been back there myself, I wrote a poem of my own about Venice; and quite aside from the more unavoidable overlappings, on rereading "The Venetian Vespers" I am now bemused to find the word *lubricities*. When I wrote of the Venetians' "lubricious throngs," was that where I got it from? I can't be sure it wasn't. My guess is that we all borrow—or steal, if we're mature enough—more than is generally recognized. My own raids on what I most admire are so frequent that I would like to think so.

One more thing I should like to say, and that is how funny Anthony Hecht can be. I read "Sestina D'Inverno" at a writers' workshop, the first I ever taught, and out of the dozens of poems to which my auditors were subjected in the course of ten days, that poem stands out as one of the few unqualified hits. It occurred to me at the time that—just as Stevens's "No

Possum, No Sop, No Taters" must be in some way a tribute to "La Belle Dame Sans Merci"—Anthony Hecht's sestina, with its tropical warmths encapsulated in the actuality of blizzards, might be seen as an updated "Eve of Saint Agnes." Whether consciously it is any such thing, I haven't yet been brave enough to ask.

An Interview

You first published a collection of poems entitled Multitudes, Multitudes *(Washington Street Press) in 1974. How marked do you find the difference between this initial collection and* The Kingfisher *(Knopf, 1983), which received such critical acclaim? Do you feel that your style changed dramatically within those nine years or, was it, instead, a question of the readers' response?*

No, I don't think my style has changed *dramatically.* I'd like to think I'd learned to be somewhat less discursive than I tended to be in *Multitudes, Multitudes;* and just possibly I've acquired a lighter touch—become, on occasion anyhow, more playful.

In what may be interpreted, perhaps, as an 'autobiographical' poem, "Imago" (The Kingfisher), a young girl, attempting to write, is chastised: "But it has no form!" Your poems, so precisely crafted, display a heightened awareness of form. Do you remember a particular moment when you felt you had made a breakthrough, finding yourself "at home" in a poem, discovering, as it were, your own voice?

Everyone who has commented on "Imago" has supposed that the objection "But it has no form!" was a comment from a mentor when I was still a student. In fact, what I was remembering was a friendly remark by a contemporary to whom I'd shown a sketch (in prose) after I'd come to New York and was finding it difficult to write anything at all. I felt that the comment was entirely justified. As a student, I don't recall any

---

Conducted by Elise Paschen for, and originally published in, *Oxford Poetry* (Winter 1986–87). Reprinted by permission.

really discouraging comments from anyone. When I wrote poetry during my teens, it had plenty of form: I could handle the sonnet quite competently, or, perhaps more precisely, the form took over all too completely. But by the time I finished college I had come to think of myself as a novelist; and the novel seems now to have been a form I couldn't handle at all. No, I don't remember anything quite so specific as feeling that I'd "found my own voice"; what happened was that, sometime in the late fifties, I sat down to write about an experience I didn't quite understand, and found myself doing it in verse rather than prose. This actually frightened me, as though I'd been taken over by some uninvited guest and told what to do—which is not at all the same as feeling "at home" with what was happening.

In the note to "Imago," you say that Hans Christian Andersen's story of the Little Mermaid "affected [you] more powerfully than anything else [you] read as a child." The sea figures prominently in your poetry and in at least one other poem, "Chichester" (What the Light Was Like), *the image of the mermaid resurfaces. Could you explain why this fairy tale exerted such a hold on your imagination as a child?*

Further than my note to "Imago," I don't think I can explain why images of water held such an attraction for me. I think there is some connection with my earliest memory (described in "The Woodlot")—of a patch of blossoming violets, which has always been associated in my mind with the look of water. It also attaches to the (improperly called) bluebells in "Botanical Nomenclature." Lately, I've been trying to write* about my earliest childhood memory of an actual body of water. I've been conscious ever since then (or so it seems in retrospect) of a wish to be near the ocean. As for the Andersen fairy tale, I think what drew me was some truthfulness about the pain of being an adult—the cost of growing up—or maybe, more accurately, the *omnipresence* of pain and sadness in being conscious at all. The mermaid in "Chichester," though, is simply

---

*In what was to be the title poem of *Westward*.

Keats's "half-hidden, like a mermaid in sea-weed"; I don't know that it would have occurred to me to introduce her otherwise. But the sea is certainly important to me. If I hadn't begun spending time on the coast of Maine, I'm not sure whether much, if any, of either *The Kingfisher* or *What the Light Was Like* would have been written. The Greeks associated water with the source of inspiration. Life came from the sea. Being in sight of it puts everything into perspective. Just now I'm living among hills, which I find mesmerizing in the same way—though whether to the same degree I'm not yet sure.

You have said that you "heard the echoes of Milton and Keats and couldn't get rid of them." Is it possible to pinpoint one poet who has most influenced you? Can you recall a particular poem or book of poems?

"The Eve of St. Agnes" was one of the poems that excited me most. It was the totality of sensation, the visual images, the extremes of heat and cold, the appeal to touch and taste, as well as the sounds of the poem, that made it unforgettable. I remember being similarly thrilled by Shakespeare's sonnet beginning "That time of year thou may'st in me behold." In college, I read "Lycidas" for the first time, and—maybe most overwhelming of all—discovered Hopkins. The poem I remember is "Pied Beauty"; I'm not sure I knew any others (it had been in an anthology) until I bought the *Poems*—the first book by any poet that I'd bought because I wanted to own it and not simply because it was assigned for a course. I think those four are the poets who influence me most to this day. More recently, I was electrified by reading Sylvia Plath. I owe a special debt to Marianne Moore; a similar but also special one to Elizabeth Bishop; and a different but quite specific one to Anthony Hecht. But I've left out many others who could be mentioned, or whom I admire intensely.

Robert Shaw has called you "America's oldest celebrated younger poet." What is your attitude towards recognition? What are the assets and the drawbacks of being commended later in life?

It's very pleasant to have had one's books published, and to hear from people who've read them: pleasanter, in fact, than I'd supposed it could be. My impression of literary people for a long time was that they paid for recognition with misery; and so I was only halfway willing to admit any real ambitions of my own. I think one is less in danger of being totally messed up by recognition if it *does* come when one is relatively well along in years—and the sudden notice I came into was near enough to being disastrous that I don't minimize the hazards at any age. (For the first time in my life I was reduced to taking antidepressants, which I hated the idea of doing, to ease the wear and tear on my closest friends—and I gather this isn't at all uncommon. But it is humiliating.) On the other hand, there is a consciousness of having only so much more time. On the whole, I regard myself as lucky.

In a recent interview, you mentioned that what you were writing in the late sixties and early seventies did not conform to the vogue then, which you called "Minimalist" poetry; that you felt you "used too many words." When you write, do you have a particular poetic unit in mind? And to what extent do you revise your poems?

It's seldom that I have any notion in advance of what form anything is going to take. Sometimes a stanza form takes shape with the first few lines: that is, a matter of line length, number of lines, rhyme scheme if any. Sometimes I change my mind about the form midway. Sometimes a stanza form will be scrapped entirely, and I'll start in all over again, without necessarily starting a new poem. I do a great deal of revising: I'd say that twenty or twenty-five retyped versions is not unusual. And I usually let a thing sit for a while after I've completed a draft; it's easier to spot what doesn't work if you come back to a thing after having put it out of your mind entirely. A good part of the revision is in getting rid of things—that oversupply of words that seems to come all too naturally. I suppose that once in a while I may sit down with a form in mind—as when I wrote that pseudo-sestina, "The Reedbeds of the Hackensack." By the time I had a hundred

161

lines of "An Anatomy of Migraine," I knew that it would be in two parts of a hundred lines each; but this was dictated by the notion of the two halves of the brain, the pairing of Tweedledum and Tweedledee, and so on. I've not often been that schematic, and I'm not sure anyone is going to care about the chiasmus that became part of the structure. I've heard from a number of people about that poem, and nobody has yet mentioned the structure: mostly they're people who're subject to migraine, or doctors who treat people who are. But that's going beyond the question.

How difficult is it to find verbal equivalents for the visual world? "What the Light Was Like" seems to address this dilemma . . .

I don't think finding verbal equivalents for the *visual* world is what is difficult; it's addressing oneself to the nonvisual, the invisible, that's the challenge. I've been thinking a lot lately about Wordsworth (I've been teaching a course about him and his circle, especially Dorothy) and am struck by his observation on the tyranny of the eye. (Possibly the great power of Milton to *envision* was made possible by his blindness. Has anyone gone into this, I wonder?) How to find verbal equivalents for physical pain, for instance; or for the effect of music. That's what I was doing in "Sunday Music," and, of course, in "Beethoven, Opus 111." I was startled when a critic, a favorable one at that, remarked that the latter poem exemplified "the fallacy of imitative form." I didn't know what he could be talking about, and I'm not sure that I still do, though I've since come across the dictum of Yvor Winters on that subject. It would seem as though finding verbal equivalents would almost necessarily entail being imitative. I don't understand critics a good deal of the time. Look at the number of people who write poems about paintings, and who do it so that one in fact *sees* the painting. That suggests to me that rendering visual impressions isn't all that difficult.

In a note to "Rain at Bellagio" you suggest: "The scheme may be clearer if this poem is thought of as a meditation in the form of a travelogue." You once wrote a travel book. Is there something unique about a place that inspires you to write about it, and why does a poem seem better suited for this type of description than prose?

If I'm asked to describe myself as a poet, what I end up saying is that I'm a poet of place. Places inspire me all the time. I don't like to think that I'm a poet of travel, but poems do certainly come out of my travels. It's a good deal easier to say something about a place that's totally unfamiliar, of course, than about a place you've known all your life. The first poems I wrote about the coast of Maine were relatively slight; I couldn't have written the title poem of *What the Light Was Like* until I'd spent some time in that particular fishing village. My effort at a travel book was based on detailed journals I'd kept; and in fact "Rain at Bellagio" came out of journal entries, set down twenty years before. I'd like to think it was a distillation, though I must have kept some phrases from the original. But it has the flavor of a travelogue, as distinguished from that of a poem of place; or at least I think it has. I don't know that any other poem of mine is as close to a prose original. Since I'm something of a nomad, and like traveling, I've done a number of travel poems. "A Procession at Candlemas" and "Witness" are about traveling by bus: "Losing Track of Language" is about traveling by train, and so is "Babel Aboard the Hellas International Express." I don't think the question of why *these* weren't written in prose would have arisen. When I kept those voluminous travel journals, I hadn't found any other form to write in. Now that I've gotten to think of myself as a poet, I don't write in prose any more, given the option, because the shape of a poem now seems to come more naturally—or maybe I should say it curbs my natural verbosity more effectively—than trying to write in prose.

You first visited England in 1949, and you stayed here during the spring of 1983. In "A Baroque Sunburst" (What the Light Was Like) you write: "you might suppose / the coast of Maine had Europe / on the brain or in its bones, as though / it were a kind of sickness." As an American raised in the Midwest, yet now an inveterate New Yorker, can you gauge this relationship between yourself and Europe (and, in particular, Great Britain)?

The importance of Europe (and of Great Britain in particular, as you rightly put it) is so great for me that I can hardly exaggerate it. My first visit to England—and in particular to Oxford, where for the first time I believed that the past could be experienced as something present—changed my life forever. The music of English poetry was already ringing in my ears; being present on the soil of England itself established a continuity that made me feel not quite such a total misfit. The Midwest may not produce any more misfits than any other region, but just about anyone with small confidence but large imagining is going to be a misfit out there. New York is, of course, full of such misfits—which makes it not the most comfortable place for any of us to settle into. Until you start thinking your own thoughts, and not just fumbling around with received ideas, it's hardly possible for anyone to be comfortable in *any* environment. The experience of traveling in Greece, some years later, carried the whole process another step. What I've only begun to do is to puzzle out what all of this means in relation to the place I came from. I think about it more and more, though I have no plans for going back there except as an intensely interested visitor.

T. S. Eliot was born in St. Louis and settled in London. Marianne Moore was born in St. Louis and settled in Brooklyn. Elizabeth Bishop began life in Nova Scotia (if I'm not mistaken) and can hardly be said to have settled anywhere. I feel a certain kinship with her nomadism, if that is what it is: though I've been based in New York for many years, I feel less and less as though I really *lived* anywhere. Is that kind of uprooting possibly an American tradition? An American writer from whom I took certain cues (having to do with solitude) was Thoreau: I can't think of another to whom I've felt closer, over the years. I feel certain affinities with Hart Crane—the side of him that felt affinities with Keats, anyhow—but don't know whether that constitutes a line of poetic descent. The more I think about this question, the more intriguing it becomes. Whatever answer there may be, I suspect, will have some relation to being native to the Midwest—and having left it. And then looking back.

How Everything Connects: Julia
Budenz, John Ashbery, and Others

Since about 1970, Julia Budenz has been at work on a long
poem. Excerpts from it have appeared in a few literary jour-
nals, and in 1984 Wesleyan University Press brought out a
volume entitled *From the Gardens of Flora Baum*, constituting no
more than two sections of Book 2, Part 5. The completed work
is to consist of five books; at the time I last inquired, there were
already more than six hundred typewritten pages—which
would mean that for sheer length such things as *Kaddish* or *The
Auroras of Autumn* have been left behind in favor of, say, *The
Faerie Queene*. A first encounter with such a work in progress is
likely to be baffling. But with each installment, and still more
with rereading, I have found newly thrilling a poem whose
design is not entirely revealed, but whose execution is wonder-
fully various, beguiling, and funny.

Critics thus far have not, however, had much to say of Julia
Budenz—for the reason, I suppose, that since she does not
write short poems, it is hard to compare her with anyone. The
often extended cadence of her lines, for example, suggests
not that she has been influenced by Whitman, but rather that
like him she has long been at home with the English Bible. An
occasional bit of word play ("And you— / Do you write /

Adapted from an essay originally published in the *Boston Review*
(October, 1986). An earlier version appeared in *Conversant Essays:
Contemporary Poets on Poetry* (Detroit: Wayne State University Press,
1990).

English / ? . . . / Sicker I do") might suggest Joyce; but not the reference to Calypso:

> She was kind to me.
> But she wanted me to forget
> The fires burning blue above
> My Ithaca. Her soft
> Words, her soft . . . .

Or to Circe:

> The schoolroom was restless
> Like a pen of navy-blue-white-collared calves,
> With big bronze eyes turned outward. Groping
> Among the bronze passages, I imparted the thread
> Which I could hardly claim to descry.
> How to fast, how to feast, how to speak, and how
> To shut up. Around us we heard
> The endless rooting and grunting.

These tell us only of a like immersion in the *Odyssey*. And perhaps it is no more than the copious botanical exactitude of a work that is, in its own mysteriously spacious and leisurely way, concerned with horticulture, which invites comparison with *Remembrance of Things Past* and its hawthorns, its chrysanthemums and cattleyas: in tone there is hardly any resemblance. Memory is evoked, certainly; but it is memory of a less idiosyncratic kind, more steadily resonant and strange. In *The Gardens of Flora Baum,* the long common memory of the classical world opens as a habitable place, along with (among others) Florida, the coast of Scotland, and the freezing thoroughfares of Cambridge, Massachusetts. It is part of a vision of how everything connects, of how it is possible at any moment to step from the everyday into the sacred, and back again.

Take, for example, Wallace Stevens, to whose work Julia Budenz would seem to owe more than a little:

> Whirlings in the gutters, whirlings
> Around and away, resembling the presence of thought,
> Resembling the presences of thoughts, as if,

In the end, the whole psychology, the self,
The town, the weather, in a casual litter,
Together, said words of the world are the life of the world.

Thus from ordinary New Haven we are taken back to Shelley's leaf-dispersing west wind, and from that to Milton's metaphor of the leaves at Vallombrosa, back to the third canto of the Inferno, to the sixth book of the *Aeneid* and to the eleventh book of the *Odyssey:* the Underworld, the fluttering multitudes whose resemblance to fallen leaves was, in the original Greek, only implicit, not yet a metaphor.

There is a kind of thinking that regards all this as a misfortune, at least for us latecomers. But I find it hard to see how such thinking can be taken very far, or very seriously. If it were, all poets would end up in the condition of the one I remember hearing publicly declare, "I want to die of my own poison"—and who since then, so far as I know, has entirely ceased to be heard from. At a polar remove from such a fate are the likes of Julia Budenz, at home in Cambridge, Massachusetts, but also with that long common memory:

> To sing of presidents and revolutions,
> Apollo chided, tapping the other shoulder,
> Crouch in your cave another twenty years,
> Piling the volumes high above your head,
> Tunneling through big books until you see
> The culmination of your drawn-out song.

Thalia, the Blossoming One, is present; the cave is hers. Or it is Plato's. Others make their appearance there from time to time. Diotima is one of them:

> She had a question:
> What do we think would happen if it happened
> To one to see the beautiful itself . . . ?
> It was Socrates again, it was Plato, it seemed for a moment
>   like Jove, I almost let go, it was a bull, bold and resolute,
> Huge, horned, garlanded, white, wide-eyed but not innocent,
>   foxy, flighty, mighty, muscular, determined, that seemed to
>   have run up from the fens

And was carrying me, back across the Charles, through
　　Roxbury, into Dorchester Bay, across the ocean, to Europe,
　　to Old Europe, where Jove was at home . . . .

Though the classical learning behind this may be excep-
tional, the nature of the presence is not. Such recurrences, if
we are to believe Harold Bloom—who calls them misreadings,
and after some resistance I now find that fair enough—are
what makes the world go round. Rereading the title poem of
A Wave, and admiring it more with each rereading, I have
come to think of it as a twentieth-century equivalent of *The
Prelude.* John Ashbery rewriting Wordsworth? Admittedly,

　　To be always articulating these preludes, there seems to be no
　　Sense in it, if it is going to be perpetually five o'clock

would appear to connect with Eliot's plural preludes rather
than Wordsworth's in the singular. But there are enough refer-
ences to such things as gibbets and waterfalls, along with so
many recurrences of the word *love* as to constitute an excess—
as one tends to find an excess of them in *The Prelude*—that
when I came to

　　Moving on we approached the top
　　Of the thing, only it was dark and no one could see,

I thought Aha!—the ascent of Mount Snowdon. The hunch
seemed confirmed, half a page later, by

　　But behind what looks like heaps of slag the peril
　　Consists in explaining everything too evenly. Those
　　Suffering from the blahs are unlikely to notice that the topic
　　Of today's lecture doesn't exist yet. . . .

There can be little doubt, in any event, that what Ashbery in
"A Wave" is wrestling with is the problem of poetic form, the
very thing that gave Wordsworth, an innovator himself, such
endless trouble. "One idea," Ashbery continues,

> is enough to organize a life and project it
> Into unusual but viable forms, but many ideas merely
> Lead one thither into a morass of their own good
>   intentions. . . .

More Wordsworthian still is the reference to

> a moan that did not issue from me
> And is pulling me back toward old forms of address
> I know I have already lived through. . . .

Recurrences, old forms of address already lived through: innovator that he was, Wordsworth lived with them too. Rereading the later books of *The Prelude,* I find not simply a history of the poet's mind but what T. S. Eliot called a fever chart, a day-to-day chronicle of ups and downs, to be read the way one reads his sister Dorothy's journals. There is that moment when the poet says—and the frankness of it is shocking—"I am lost." One thinks of Rilke's "Who, if I cried out, would hear among the angelic orders?" Such admissions of bewilderment must account for an assertion which used to puzzle me, that Wordsworth is the first modern poet. The multiple crises of those last books—loss of confidence, loss of his bearings as an individual—may be modern; but their antecedents are classical. Looking about for guidance, as Dante had done, Wordsworth found no Virgil; but he did find Coleridge, and when one thinks of their friendship, Dorothy becomes a kind of Beatrice. Having made that connection, one has to conclude that Wordsworth, this innovator, this prototypically modern poet, is nevertheless the author of a classical epic, whose central episode goes underground—becomes yet another version of the descent into hell.

Why do I find this discovered connection so thrilling? One might as well ask Julia Budenz the same about Thalia's cave. Or Wallace Stevens about the tercets of "An Ordinary Evening in New Haven." Buried though they may be, the connections, the predecessors are there and not to be denied.

UNDER DISCUSSION
Donald Hall, General Editor

Volumes in the Under Discussion series collect reviews and essays about individual poets. The series is concerned with contemporary American and English poets about whom the consensus has not yet been formed and the final vote has not been taken. Titles in the series include:

Forthcoming volumes will examine the work of Langston Hughes, Muriel Rukeyser, H.D., and Denise Levertov, among others.

Please write for further information on available editions and current prices.

Ann Arbor **The University of Michigan Press**

ACH 4567   11/20/91

PS
121
C5
1991